Gifts from a Jar
Christmas Treats

Memorable Gift Giving 2
Merry Mocha 3
Rich & Creamy Cocoa 9
Festive Cranberry Waffles 15
Lemony Poppy Seed Muffins 21
Pumpkin Spice Mini Muffins 27
Luscious Orange Cranberry Scones 33
Eggnog Cherry Quick Bread 39
Elegant Pecan Brandy Cake 45
Mistletoe Kiss Me Cakes 51
Cherry Pistachio Biscotti 57
Blissful Chocolate Biscotti 63
Snowy Date Nut Squares 69
Elfin Toffee Coffee Shortbread 75
Joyful Apricot Almond Bars 81
Fudgy Chocolate-Amaretti Brownies 87
Toasty Rosemary Nuts 93
Jolly Party Mix 99
Glorious Sugared Nuts 105
Yuletide Cheddar Crisps 111
Santa's Peppermint Chocolates 117
Crispy Holiday Treats 123

Memorable Gift Giving

Create an unforgettable holiday gift for your friends and family by giving them a homemade gift jar filled with ingredients to make festive quick breads, cakes, cookies, snacks and candy. Fill the jars as directed and add your personal decorating touch. The result—a beautiful gift that will make a lasting impression. Since most of the ingredients are premeasured and in the jar, recipe preparation is easier and more fun.

Keep the following tips in mind when preparing your gift jars.

- Always use a food-safe jar or container with an airtight lid.
- Make sure the jar or container is completely dry before filling it with ingredients.
- Use the jar size called for in the recipe.
- Measure all the ingredients accurately.
- For ease in filling, use a canning funnel, if available and a ¼-cup dry measuring cup.
- For a more attractive jar, follow the layering suggested in the recipe.
- Fill several jars at once for a make-ahead gift that can be stored until needed.
- After the jar is filled, tear out the corresponding gift tag from the book with the recipe and preparation instructions. Cover the top of the jar with a 9- or 10-inch circle of fabric. Tie the fabric and the gift tag onto the jar with raffia, ribbon, satin cord, string, yarn or lace.

Merry Mocha Mix

½ cup nonfat dry milk powder
¼ cup instant coffee granules
½ cup powdered nondairy creamer
3 tablespoons unsweetened cocoa powder
6 tablespoons granulated sugar
2 tablespoons packed brown sugar
⅛ teaspoon salt
¼ teaspoon ground nutmeg
4 to 8 cinnamon sticks

1. Layer all ingredients except cinnamon sticks in the order listed above in 1-pint food storage jar with tight-fitting lid. Lightly pack ingredients down before adding another layer.

2. Cover top of jar with fabric; attach gift tag and cinnamon sticks with raffia or ribbon.

Makes 1 (1-pint) jar

Merry Mocha

1 jar Merry Mocha Mix
6 cups water
Whipped cream

1. Remove cinnamon sticks. Place contents of jar in large saucepan. Add water. Bring to a boil, stirring to dissolve. Keep warm over low heat.
2. Pour into individual coffee cups. Stir with cinnamon stick; garnish with dollop of whipped cream.

Makes 8 (¾-cup) servings

Serving Suggestions: Sprinkle toffee baking bits over whipped cream. Or, add 1 to 2 tablespoons coffee-flavored liqueur to each cup mocha.

Single Serving: Stir Merry Mocha Mix in jar until well blended. Place ¼ cup mix in coffee cup; add ¾ cup boiling water. Stir with cinnamon stick until mix is dissolved. Garnish with dollop of whipped cream. If using large coffee mugs, double the recipe for single serving.

Merry Mocha

1 jar Merry Mocha Mix
6 cups water

Whipped cream

1. Remove cinnamon sticks. Place contents of jar in large saucepan. Add water. Bring to a boil, stirring to dissolve. Keep warm over low heat.

2. Pour into individual coffee cups. Stir with cinnamon stick; garnish with dollop of whipped cream.

Makes 8 (¾-cup) servings

Serving Suggestions: Sprinkle toffee baking bits over whipped cream. Or, add 1 to 2 tablespoons coffee-flavored liqueur to each cup mocha.

Single Serving: Stir Merry Mocha Mix in jar until well blended. Place ¼ cup mix in coffee cup; add ¾ cup boiling water. Stir with cinnamon stick until mix is dissolved. Garnish with dollop of whipped cream. If using large coffee mugs, double the recipe for single serving.

Merry Mocha

1 jar Merry Mocha Mix
6 cups water

Whipped cream

1. Remove cinnamon sticks. Place contents of jar in large saucepan. Add water. Bring to a boil, stirring to dissolve. Keep warm over low heat.

2. Pour into individual coffee cups. Stir with cinnamon stick; garnish with dollop of whipped cream.

Makes 8 (¾-cup) servings

Serving Suggestions: Sprinkle toffee baking bits over whipped cream. Or, add 1 to 2 tablespoons coffee-flavored liqueur to each cup mocha.

Single Serving: Stir Merry Mocha Mix in jar until well blended. Place ¼ cup mix in coffee cup; add ¾ cup boiling water. Stir with cinnamon stick until mix is dissolved. Garnish with dollop of whipped cream. If using large coffee mugs, double the recipe for single serving.

Merry Mocha

1 jar Merry Mocha Mix
6 cups water

Whipped cream

1. Remove cinnamon sticks. Place contents of jar in large saucepan. Add water. Bring to a boil, stirring to dissolve. Keep warm over low heat.

2. Pour into individual coffee cups. Stir with cinnamon stick; garnish with dollop of whipped cream.

Makes 8 (¾-cup) servings

Serving Suggestions: Sprinkle toffee baking bits over whipped cream. Or, add 1 to 2 tablespoons coffee-flavored liqueur to each cup mocha.

Single Serving: Stir Merry Mocha Mix in jar until well blended. Place ¼ cup mix in coffee cup; add ¾ cup boiling water. Stir with cinnamon stick until mix is dissolved. Garnish with dollop of whipped cream. If using large coffee mugs, double the recipe for single serving.

Merry Mocha

1 jar Merry Mocha Mix
6 cups water
Whipped cream

1. Remove cinnamon sticks. Place contents of jar in large saucepan. Add water. Bring to a boil, stirring to dissolve. Keep warm over low heat.

2. Pour into individual coffee cups. Stir with cinnamon stick; garnish with dollop of whipped cream.

Makes 8 (¾-cup) servings

Serving Suggestions: Sprinkle toffee baking bits over whipped cream. Or, add 1 to 2 tablespoons coffee-flavored liqueur to each cup mocha.

Single Serving: Stir Merry Mocha Mix in jar until well blended. Place ¼ cup mix in coffee cup; add ¾ cup boiling water. Stir with cinnamon stick until mix is dissolved. Garnish with dollop of whipped cream. If using large coffee mugs, double the recipe for single serving.

Merry Mocha

1 jar Merry Mocha Mix
6 cups water
Whipped cream

1. Remove cinnamon sticks. Place contents of jar in large saucepan. Add water. Bring to a boil, stirring to dissolve. Keep warm over low heat.

2. Pour into individual coffee cups. Stir with cinnamon stick; garnish with dollop of whipped cream.

Makes 8 (¾-cup) servings

Serving Suggestions: Sprinkle toffee baking bits over whipped cream. Or, add 1 to 2 tablespoons coffee-flavored liqueur to each cup mocha.

Single Serving: Stir Merry Mocha Mix in jar until well blended. Place ¼ cup mix in coffee cup; add ¾ cup boiling water. Stir with cinnamon stick until mix is dissolved. Garnish with dollop of whipped cream. If using large coffee mugs, double the recipe for single serving.

Merry Mocha

1 jar Merry Mocha Mix
6 cups water
Whipped cream

1. Remove cinnamon sticks. Place contents of jar in large saucepan. Add water. Bring to a boil, stirring to dissolve. Keep warm over low heat.

2. Pour into individual coffee cups. Stir with cinnamon stick; garnish with dollop of whipped cream.

Makes 8 (¾-cup) servings

Serving Suggestions: Sprinkle toffee baking bits over whipped cream. Or, add 1 to 2 tablespoons coffee-flavored liqueur to each cup mocha.

Single Serving: Stir Merry Mocha Mix in jar until well blended. Place ¼ cup mix in coffee cup; add ¾ cup boiling water. Stir with cinnamon stick until mix is dissolved. Garnish with dollop of whipped cream. If using large coffee mugs, double the recipe for single serving.

Rich & Creamy Cocoa Mix

¾ cup powdered nondairy creamer
½ cup nonfat dry milk powder
½ cup milk chocolate chips
¼ cup granulated sugar
¼ cup packed brown sugar
3 tablespoons unsweetened cocoa powder
⅛ teaspoon salt
8 peppermint sticks

1. Combine all ingredients in bowl except peppermint sticks; mix well. Put mix in 1-pint food storage jar with tight-fitting lid. Lightly pack mixture down, if needed. Evenly place peppermint sticks around inside of jar or tie sticks to outside of jar with ribbon.
2. Cover top of jar with fabric; attach gift tag with raffia or ribbon.

Makes 1 (1-pint) jar

Gift-Giving Tip

Line a gift basket with decorative napkins or tea towels. Add a jar of Rich & Creamy Cocoa Mix and holiday coffee mugs. Pop in a refrigerated can of aerosol whipped cream at the last minute.

Rich & Creamy Cocoa

1 jar Rich & Creamy Cocoa Mix
6 cups boiling water
Whipped cream

1. Remove peppermint sticks from jar. Place cocoa mix in medium saucepan. Add water; stir until mix is dissolved and chips are melted. Keep warm over low heat.

2. Pour into individual coffee cups. Add 1 peppermint stick to each cup; garnish with dollop of whipped cream.

Makes 8 (¾-cup) servings

Single Serving: Place ¼ cup cocoa mix in coffee cup; add ¾ cup boiling water. Stir with peppermint stick until mix is dissolved and chocolate chips are melted. Garnish with dollop of whipped cream. If using large coffee mugs, double the recipe for single serving.

Rich & Creamy Cocoa

1 jar Rich & Creamy Cocoa Mix
6 cups boiling water
Whipped cream

1. Remove peppermint sticks from jar. Place cocoa mix in medium saucepan. Add water; stir until mix is dissolved and chips are melted. Keep warm over low heat.

2. Pour into individual coffee cups. Add 1 peppermint stick to each cup ; garnish with dollop of whipped cream.

Makes 8 (¾-cup) servings

Single Serving: Place ¼ cup cocoa mix in coffee cup; add ¾ cup boiling water. Stir with peppermint stick until mix is dissolved and chocolate chips are melted. Garnish with dollop of whipped cream. If using large coffee mugs, double the recipe for single serving.

Rich & Creamy Cocoa

1 jar Rich & Creamy Cocoa Mix
6 cups boiling water
Whipped cream

1. Remove peppermint sticks from jar. Place cocoa mix in medium saucepan. Add water; stir until mix is dissolved and chips are melted. Keep warm over low heat.

2. Pour into individual coffee cups. Add 1 peppermint stick to each cup ; garnish with dollop of whipped cream.

Makes 8 (¾-cup) servings

Single Serving: Place ¼ cup cocoa mix in coffee cup; add ¾ cup boiling water. Stir with peppermint stick until mix is dissolved and chocolate chips are melted. Garnish with dollop of whipped cream. If using large coffee mugs, double the recipe for single serving.

Rich & Creamy Cocoa

1 jar Rich & Creamy Cocoa Mix
6 cups boiling water
Whipped cream

1. Remove peppermint sticks from jar. Place cocoa mix in medium saucepan. Add water; stir until mix is dissolved and chips are melted. Keep warm over low heat.

2. Pour into individual coffee cups. Add 1 peppermint stick to each cup ; garnish with dollop of whipped cream.

Makes 8 (¾-cup) servings

Single Serving: Place ¼ cup cocoa mix in coffee cup; add ¾ cup boiling water. Stir with peppermint stick until mix is dissolved and chocolate chips are melted. Garnish with dollop of whipped cream. If using large coffee mugs, double the recipe for single serving.

Rich & Creamy Cocoa

1 jar Rich & Creamy Cocoa Mix
6 cups boiling water
Whipped cream

1. Remove peppermint sticks from jar. Place cocoa mix in medium saucepan. Add water; stir until mix is dissolved and chips are melted. Keep warm over low heat.

2. Pour into individual coffee cups. Add 1 peppermint stick to each cup ; garnish with dollop of whipped cream.

Makes 8 ($\frac{3}{4}$-cup) servings

Single Serving: Place $\frac{1}{4}$ cup cocoa mix in coffee cup; add $\frac{3}{4}$ cup boiling water. Stir with peppermint stick until mix is dissolved and chocolate chips are melted. Garnish with dollop of whipped cream. If using large coffee mugs, double the recipe for single serving.

Rich & Creamy Cocoa

1 jar Rich & Creamy Cocoa Mix
6 cups boiling water
Whipped cream

1. Remove peppermint sticks from jar. Place cocoa mix in medium saucepan. Add water; stir until mix is dissolved and chips are melted. Keep warm over low heat.

2. Pour into individual coffee cups. Add 1 peppermint stick to each cup ; garnish with dollop of whipped cream.

Makes 8 ($\frac{3}{4}$-cup) servings

Single Serving: Place $\frac{1}{4}$ cup cocoa mix in coffee cup; add $\frac{3}{4}$ cup boiling water. Stir with peppermint stick until mix is dissolved and chocolate chips are melted. Garnish with dollop of whipped cream. If using large coffee mugs, double the recipe for single serving.

Rich & Creamy Cocoa

1 jar Rich & Creamy Cocoa Mix
6 cups boiling water
Whipped cream

1. Remove peppermint sticks from jar. Place cocoa mix in medium saucepan. Add water; stir until mix is dissolved and chips are melted. Keep warm over low heat.

2. Pour into individual coffee cups. Add 1 peppermint stick to each cup ; garnish with dollop of whipped cream.

Makes 8 ($\frac{3}{4}$-cup) servings

Single Serving: Place $\frac{1}{4}$ cup cocoa mix in coffee cup; add $\frac{3}{4}$ cup boiling water. Stir with peppermint stick until mix is dissolved and chocolate chips are melted. Garnish with dollop of whipped cream. If using large coffee mugs, double the recipe for single serving.

Festive Cranberry Waffle Mix

¾ cup all-purpose flour
2 teaspoons baking powder
1 teaspoon dried orange peel
½ teaspoon baking soda
½ teaspoon ground cinnamon
¼ teaspoon salt
⅓ cup yellow cornmeal
⅓ cup sugar
½ cup dried cranberries or dried cherries, coarsely chopped
¼ cup all-purpose flour

1. Layer all ingredients in the order listed above in 1-pint food storage jar with tight-fitting lid. Lightly pack down ingredients before adding another layer.

2. Cover top of jar with fabric; attach gift tag with raffia or ribbon.

Makes 1 (1-pint) jar

Festive Cranberry Waffles

1 jar Festive Cranberry Waffle Mix
1 cup buttermilk
¼ to ½ cup milk or orange juice, divided
1 egg
1 teaspoon vanilla
3 tablespoons butter, melted
Powdered sugar, butter and maple syrup

Preheat waffle iron. Place contents of jar in large bowl; stir until well blended. Whisk together buttermilk, ¼ cup milk, egg and vanilla in medium bowl. Add to flour mixture; stir until just moistened. Stir in butter. Add additional milk, 1 tablespoon at a time, if batter is too thick. Spray waffle iron with nonstick cooking spray. Spoon about ¾ cup batter* onto iron. Close lid; bake until steaming stops or waffles are brown and crispy. Serve with powdered sugar, butter and maple syrup. *Makes 4 (7-inch) round waffles*

*Check the manufacturer's directions for recommended amount of batter and baking time.

Serving Suggestion: Combine 1 cup mascarpone cheese, ¼ cup maple syrup and 1 teaspoon vanilla until well mixed. Serve in place of butter and syrup. Yum!

Tip: When making waffles for a crowd, keep the waffles warm in a preheated 200°F oven by placing them on the oven rack in a single layer. Heat the plates on another rack. The waffles will be warm and delicious.

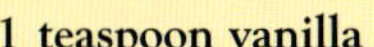

Festive Cranberry Waffles

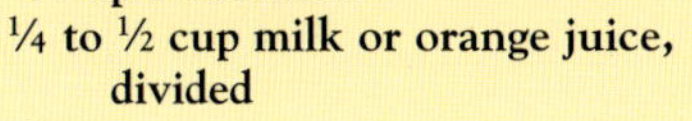

1 jar Festive Cranberry Waffle Mix
1 cup buttermilk
¼ to ½ cup milk or orange juice, divided
1 egg

1 teaspoon vanilla
3 tablespoons butter, melted
Powdered sugar, butter and maple syrup

Preheat waffle iron. Place contents of jar in large bowl; stir until well blended. Whisk together buttermilk, ¼ cup milk, egg and vanilla in medium bowl. Add to flour mixture; stir until just moistened. Stir in butter. Add additional milk, 1 tablespoon at a time, if batter is too thick. Spray waffle iron with nonstick cooking spray. Spoon about ¾ cup batter* onto iron. Close lid; bake until steaming stops or waffles are brown and crispy. Serve with powdered sugar, butter and maple syrup. *Makes 4 (7-inch) round waffles*

*Check the manufacturer's directions for recommended amount of batter and baking time.

Serving Suggestion: Combine 1 cup mascarpone cheese, ¼ cup maple syrup and 1 teaspoon vanilla until well mixed. Serve in place of butter and syrup. Yum!

Festive Cranberry Waffles

1 jar Festive Cranberry Waffle Mix
1 cup buttermilk
¼ to ½ cup milk or orange juice, divided
1 egg
1 teaspoon vanilla
3 tablespoons butter, melted
Powdered sugar, butter and maple syrup

Preheat waffle iron. Place contents of jar in large bowl; stir until well blended. Whisk together buttermilk, ¼ cup milk, egg and vanilla in medium bowl. Add to flour mixture; stir until just moistened. Stir in butter. Add additional milk, 1 tablespoon at a time, if batter is too thick. Spray waffle iron with nonstick cooking spray. Spoon about ¾ cup batter* onto iron. Close lid; bake until steaming stops or waffles are brown and crispy. Serve with powdered sugar, butter and maple syrup. *Makes 4 (7-inch) round waffles*

*Check the manufacturer's directions for recommended amount of batter and baking time.

Serving Suggestion: Combine 1 cup mascarpone cheese, ¼ cup maple syrup and 1 teaspoon vanilla until well mixed. Serve in place of butter and syrup. Yum!

Festive Cranberry Waffles

1 jar Festive Cranberry Waffle Mix
1 cup buttermilk
¼ to ½ cup milk or orange juice, divided
1 egg
1 teaspoon vanilla
3 tablespoons butter, melted
Powdered sugar, butter and maple syrup

Preheat waffle iron. Place contents of jar in large bowl; stir until well blended. Whisk together buttermilk, ¼ cup milk, egg and vanilla in medium bowl. Add to flour mixture; stir until just moistened. Stir in butter. Add additional milk, 1 tablespoon at a time, if batter is too thick. Spray waffle iron with nonstick cooking spray. Spoon about ¾ cup batter* onto iron. Close lid; bake until steaming stops or waffles are brown and crispy. Serve with powdered sugar, butter and maple syrup. *Makes 4 (7-inch) round waffles*

*Check the manufacturer's directions for recommended amount of batter and baking time.

Serving Suggestion: Combine 1 cup mascarpone cheese, ¼ cup maple syrup and 1 teaspoon vanilla until well mixed. Serve in place of butter and syrup. Yum!

Festive Cranberry Waffles

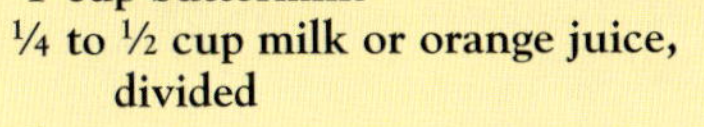

- 1 jar Festive Cranberry Waffle Mix
- 1 cup buttermilk
- ¼ to ½ cup milk or orange juice, divided
- 1 egg
- 1 teaspoon vanilla
- 3 tablespoons butter, melted
- Powdered sugar, butter and maple syrup

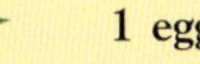

Preheat waffle iron. Place contents of jar in large bowl; stir until well blended. Whisk together buttermilk, ¼ cup milk, egg and vanilla in medium bowl. Add to flour mixture; stir until just moistened. Stir in butter. Add additional milk, 1 tablespoon at a time, if batter is too thick. Spray waffle iron with nonstick cooking spray. Spoon about ¾ cup batter* onto iron. Close lid; bake until steaming stops or waffles are brown and crispy. Serve with powdered sugar, butter and maple syrup. *Makes 4 (7-inch) round waffles*

*Check the manufacturer's directions for recommended amount of batter and baking time.

Serving Suggestion: Combine 1 cup mascarpone cheese, ¼ cup maple syrup and 1 teaspoon vanilla until well mixed. Serve in place of butter and syrup. Yum!

Festive Cranberry Waffles

- 1 jar Festive Cranberry Waffle Mix
- 1 cup buttermilk
- ¼ to ½ cup milk or orange juice, divided
- 1 egg
- 1 teaspoon vanilla
- 3 tablespoons butter, melted
- Powdered sugar, butter and maple syrup

Preheat waffle iron. Place contents of jar in large bowl; stir until well blended. Whisk together buttermilk, ¼ cup milk, egg and vanilla in medium bowl. Add to flour mixture; stir until just moistened. Stir in butter. Add additional milk, 1 tablespoon at a time, if batter is too thick. Spray waffle iron with nonstick cooking spray. Spoon about ¾ cup batter* onto iron. Close lid; bake until steaming stops or waffles are brown and crispy. Serve with powdered sugar, butter and maple syrup. *Makes 4 (7-inch) round waffles*

*Check the manufacturer's directions for recommended amount of batter and baking time.

Serving Suggestion: Combine 1 cup mascarpone cheese, ¼ cup maple syrup and 1 teaspoon vanilla until well mixed. Serve in place of butter and syrup. Yum!

Festive Cranberry Waffles

- 1 jar Festive Cranberry Waffle Mix
- 1 cup buttermilk
- ¼ to ½ cup milk or orange juice, divided
- 1 egg
- 1 teaspoon vanilla
- 3 tablespoons butter, melted
- Powdered sugar, butter and maple syrup

Preheat waffle iron. Place contents of jar in large bowl; stir until well blended. Whisk together buttermilk, ¼ cup milk, egg and vanilla in medium bowl. Add to flour mixture; stir until just moistened. Stir in butter. Add additional milk, 1 tablespoon at a time, if batter is too thick. Spray waffle iron with nonstick cooking spray. Spoon about ¾ cup batter* onto iron. Close lid; bake until steaming stops or waffles are brown and crispy. Serve with powdered sugar, butter and maple syrup. *Makes 4 (7-inch) round waffles*

*Check the manufacturer's directions for recommended amount of batter and baking time.

Serving Suggestion: Combine 1 cup mascarpone cheese, ¼ cup maple syrup and 1 teaspoon vanilla until well mixed. Serve in place of butter and syrup. Yum!

Lemony Poppy Seed Muffin Mix

1 cup all-purpose flour
½ cup yellow cornmeal
3 tablespoons poppy seeds
¾ cup granulated sugar
½ cup packed brown sugar
1 cup all-purpose flour
2 teaspoons baking powder
½ teaspoon baking soda
½ teaspoon salt
¼ cup powdered sugar

1. Layer all ingredients except powdered sugar in the order listed above in 1-quart food storage jar with tight-fitting lid. Lightly pack down ingredients before adding another layer. Place powdered sugar in small plastic food storage bag. Close with twist tie; cut off top of bag. Place bag in jar.

2. Cover top of jar with fabric; attach gift tag with raffia or ribbon.

Makes 1 (1-quart) jar

Lemony Poppy Seed Muffins

1 jar Lemony Poppy Seed Muffin Mix
½ cup plus 1 teaspoon fresh lemon juice (2 lemons), divided
½ cup oil
2 eggs
2 teaspoons grated lemon peel

1. Preheat oven to 375°F. Spray 12 regular-size (2½-inch) muffin cups with nonstick cooking spray.

2. Remove powdered sugar packet from jar. Place remaining contents of jar in large bowl; stir until well blended. Whisk together ½ cup lemon juice, oil, eggs and lemon peel in medium bowl until well blended. Add to muffin mixture; stir just until moistened. Spoon evenly into prepared muffin cups, filling each cup ¾ full.

3. Bake 15 to 20 minutes or until toothpick inserted into centers comes out clean. Remove muffins to wire racks. Mix powdered sugar with remaining 1 teaspoon lemon juice to make glaze. Drizzle over warm muffins.

Makes 12 muffins

Lemony Poppy Seed Muffins

1 jar Lemony Poppy Seed Muffin Mix
½ cup plus 1 teaspoon fresh lemon juice (2 lemons), divided
½ cup oil
2 eggs
2 teaspoons grated lemon peel

1. Preheat oven to 375°F. Spray 12 regular-size (2½-inch) muffin cups with nonstick cooking spray.

2. Remove powdered sugar packet from jar. Place remaining contents of jar in large bowl; stir until well blended. Whisk together ½ cup lemon juice, oil, eggs and lemon peel in medium bowl until well blended. Add to muffin mixture; stir just until moistened. Spoon evenly into prepared muffin cups, filling each cup ¾ full.

3. Bake 15 to 20 minutes or until toothpick inserted into centers comes out clean. Remove muffins to wire racks. Mix powdered sugar with remaining 1 teaspoon lemon juice to make glaze. Drizzle over warm muffins. *Makes 12 muffins*

Lemony Poppy Seed Muffins

1 jar Lemony Poppy Seed Muffin Mix
½ cup plus 1 teaspoon fresh lemon juice (2 lemons), divided
½ cup oil
2 eggs
2 teaspoons grated lemon peel

1. Preheat oven to 375°F. Spray 12 regular-size (2½-inch) muffin cups with nonstick cooking spray.

2. Remove powdered sugar packet from jar. Place remaining contents of jar in large bowl; stir until well blended. Whisk together ½ cup lemon juice, oil, eggs and lemon peel in medium bowl until well blended. Add to muffin mixture; stir just until moistened. Spoon evenly into prepared muffin cups, filling each cup ¾ full.

3. Bake 15 to 20 minutes or until toothpick inserted into centers comes out clean. Remove muffins to wire racks. Mix powdered sugar with remaining 1 teaspoon lemon juice to make glaze. Drizzle over warm muffins. *Makes 12 muffins*

Lemony Poppy Seed Muffins

1 jar Lemony Poppy Seed Muffin Mix
½ cup plus 1 teaspoon fresh lemon juice (2 lemons), divided
½ cup oil
2 eggs
2 teaspoons grated lemon peel

1. Preheat oven to 375°F. Spray 12 regular-size (2½-inch) muffin cups with nonstick cooking spray.

2. Remove powdered sugar packet from jar. Place remaining contents of jar in large bowl; stir until well blended. Whisk together ½ cup lemon juice, oil, eggs and lemon peel in medium bowl until well blended. Add to muffin mixture; stir just until moistened. Spoon evenly into prepared muffin cups, filling each cup ¾ full.

3. Bake 15 to 20 minutes or until toothpick inserted into centers comes out clean. Remove muffins to wire racks. Mix powdered sugar with remaining 1 teaspoon lemon juice to make glaze. Drizzle over warm muffins. *Makes 12 muffins*

Lemony Poppy Seed Muffins

1 jar Lemony Poppy Seed Muffin Mix
½ cup plus 1 teaspoon fresh lemon juice (2 lemons), divided
½ cup oil
2 eggs
2 teaspoons grated lemon peel

1. Preheat oven to 375°F. Spray 12 regular-size (2½-inch) muffin cups with nonstick cooking spray.

2. Remove powdered sugar packet from jar. Place remaining contents of jar in large bowl; stir until well blended. Whisk together ½ cup lemon juice, oil, eggs and lemon peel in medium bowl until well blended. Add to muffin mixture; stir just until moistened. Spoon evenly into prepared muffin cups, filling each cup ¾ full.

3. Bake 15 to 20 minutes or until toothpick inserted into centers comes out clean. Remove muffins to wire racks. Mix powdered sugar with remaining 1 teaspoon lemon juice to make glaze. Drizzle over warm muffins. *Makes 12 muffins*

Lemony Poppy Seed Muffins

1 jar Lemony Poppy Seed Muffin Mix
½ cup plus 1 teaspoon fresh lemon juice (2 lemons), divided
½ cup oil
2 eggs
2 teaspoons grated lemon peel

1. Preheat oven to 375°F. Spray 12 regular-size (2½-inch) muffin cups with nonstick cooking spray.

2. Remove powdered sugar packet from jar. Place remaining contents of jar in large bowl; stir until well blended. Whisk together ½ cup lemon juice, oil, eggs and lemon peel in medium bowl until well blended. Add to muffin mixture; stir just until moistened. Spoon evenly into prepared muffin cups, filling each cup ¾ full.

3. Bake 15 to 20 minutes or until toothpick inserted into centers comes out clean. Remove muffins to wire racks. Mix powdered sugar with remaining 1 teaspoon lemon juice to make glaze. Drizzle over warm muffins. *Makes 12 muffins*

Lemony Poppy Seed Muffins

1 jar Lemony Poppy Seed Muffin Mix
½ cup plus 1 teaspoon fresh lemon juice (2 lemons), divided
½ cup oil
2 eggs
2 teaspoons grated lemon peel

1. Preheat oven to 375°F. Spray 12 regular-size (2½-inch) muffin cups with nonstick cooking spray.

2. Remove powdered sugar packet from jar. Place remaining contents of jar in large bowl; stir until well blended. Whisk together ½ cup lemon juice, oil, eggs and lemon peel in medium bowl until well blended. Add to muffin mixture; stir just until moistened. Spoon evenly into prepared muffin cups, filling each cup ¾ full.

3. Bake 15 to 20 minutes or until toothpick inserted into centers comes out clean. Remove muffins to wire racks. Mix powdered sugar with remaining 1 teaspoon lemon juice to make glaze. Drizzle over warm muffins. *Makes 12 muffins*

Pumpkin Spice Mini Muffin Mix

- 2 cups all-purpose flour
- 2 teaspoons baking powder
- ¾ teaspoon salt
- ½ teaspoon baking soda
- ½ teaspoon ground ginger
- ¼ teaspoon ground nutmeg
- ¼ teaspoon ground cloves
- ¾ cup chopped dried cranberries
- ½ cup brown sugar
- ¼ cup granulated sugar
- 1 teaspoon ground cinnamon

1. Layer all ingredients except granulated sugar and cinnamon in the order listed above in 1-quart food storage jar with tight-fitting lid. Place granulated sugar and cinnamon in small plastic food storage bag. Close with twist tie; cut off top of bag. Place bag in jar.
2. Cover top of jar with fabric; attach gift tag with raffia or ribbon.

Makes 1 (1-quart) jar

Pumpkin Spice Mini Muffins

1 jar Pumpkin Spice Mini Muffin Mix
½ cup (1 stick) butter, softened
1 cup solid pack pumpkin
2 eggs
½ cup orange juice
1 teaspoon vanilla

1. Preheat oven to 400°F. Grease or paper line 36 mini (1¾-inch) or 12 regular-size (2½-inch) muffin cups. Remove cinnamon sugar packet from jar. Place contents of jar in large bowl; stir until well blended. Beat butter in medium bowl with electric mixer on medium speed until creamy. Beat in pumpkin, eggs, orange juice and vanilla until well blended. (Mixture may appear curdled.) Add to flour mixture; stir until just moistened. Spoon evenly into prepared muffin cups, filling each cup ¾ full.

2. Bake 12 to 15 minutes or until toothpick inserted into centers comes out clean. Remove muffins from pans. Place cinnamon sugar in small bowl. Roll warm muffins in sugar. Serve immediately.

Makes 36 miniature-size or 12 regular-size muffins

Pumpkin Spice Mini Muffins

- 1 jar Pumpkin Spice Mini Muffin Mix
- ½ cup (1 stick) butter, softened
- 1 cup solid pack pumpkin
- 2 eggs
- ½ cup orange juice
- 1 teaspoon vanilla

1. Preheat oven to 400°F. Grease or paper line 36 mini (1¾-inch) or 12 regular-size (2½-inch) muffin cups. Remove cinnamon sugar packet from jar. Place contents of jar in large bowl; stir until well blended. Beat butter in medium bowl with electric mixer on medium speed until creamy. Beat in pumpkin, eggs, orange juice and vanilla until well blended. (Mixture may appear curdled.) Add to flour mixture; stir until just moistened. Spoon evenly into prepared muffin cups, filling each cup ¾ full.

2. Bake 12 to 15 minutes or until toothpick inserted into centers comes out clean. Remove muffins from pans. Place cinnamon sugar in small bowl. Roll warm muffins in sugar. Serve immediately. *Makes 36 miniature-size or 12 regular-size muffins*

Pumpkin Spice Mini Muffins

- 1 jar Pumpkin Spice Mini Muffin Mix
- ½ cup (1 stick) butter, softened
- 1 cup solid pack pumpkin
- 2 eggs
- ½ cup orange juice
- 1 teaspoon vanilla

1. Preheat oven to 400°F. Grease or paper line 36 mini (1¾-inch) or 12 regular-size (2½-inch) muffin cups. Remove cinnamon sugar packet from jar. Place contents of jar in large bowl; stir until well blended. Beat butter in medium bowl with electric mixer on medium speed until creamy. Beat in pumpkin, eggs, orange juice and vanilla until well blended. (Mixture may appear curdled.) Add to flour mixture; stir until just moistened. Spoon evenly into prepared muffin cups, filling each cup ¾ full.

2. Bake 12 to 15 minutes or until toothpick inserted into centers comes out clean. Remove muffins from pans. Place cinnamon sugar in small bowl. Roll warm muffins in sugar. Serve immediately. *Makes 36 miniature-size or 12 regular-size muffins*

Pumpkin Spice Mini Muffins

- 1 jar Pumpkin Spice Mini Muffin Mix
- ½ cup (1 stick) butter, softened
- 1 cup solid pack pumpkin
- 2 eggs
- ½ cup orange juice
- 1 teaspoon vanilla

1. Preheat oven to 400°F. Grease or paper line 36 mini (1¾-inch) or 12 regular-size (2½-inch) muffin cups. Remove cinnamon sugar packet from jar. Place contents of jar in large bowl; stir until well blended. Beat butter in medium bowl with electric mixer on medium speed until creamy. Beat in pumpkin, eggs, orange juice and vanilla until well blended. (Mixture may appear curdled.) Add to flour mixture; stir until just moistened. Spoon evenly into prepared muffin cups, filling each cup ¾ full.

2. Bake 12 to 15 minutes or until toothpick inserted into centers comes out clean. Remove muffins from pans. Place cinnamon sugar in small bowl. Roll warm muffins in sugar. Serve immediately. *Makes 36 miniature-size or 12 regular-size muffins*

Pumpkin Spice Mini Muffins

1 jar Pumpkin Spice Mini Muffin Mix
½ cup (1 stick) butter, softened
1 cup solid pack pumpkin
2 eggs
½ cup orange juice
1 teaspoon vanilla

1. Preheat oven to 400°F. Grease or paper line 36 mini (1¾-inch) or 12 regular-size (2½-inch) muffin cups. Remove cinnamon sugar packet from jar. Place contents of jar in large bowl; stir until well blended. Beat butter in medium bowl with electric mixer on medium speed until creamy. Beat in pumpkin, eggs, orange juice and vanilla until well blended. (Mixture may appear curdled.) Add to flour mixture; stir until just moistened. Spoon evenly into prepared muffin cups, filling each cup ¾ full.

2. Bake 12 to 15 minutes or until toothpick inserted into centers comes out clean. Remove muffins from pans. Place cinnamon sugar in small bowl. Roll warm muffins in sugar. Serve immediately. *Makes 36 miniature-size or 12 regular-size muffins*

Pumpkin Spice Mini Muffins

1 jar Pumpkin Spice Mini Muffin Mix
½ cup (1 stick) butter, softened
1 cup solid pack pumpkin
2 eggs
½ cup orange juice
1 teaspoon vanilla

1. Preheat oven to 400°F. Grease or paper line 36 mini (1¾-inch) or 12 regular-size (2½-inch) muffin cups. Remove cinnamon sugar packet from jar. Place contents of jar in large bowl; stir until well blended. Beat butter in medium bowl with electric mixer on medium speed until creamy. Beat in pumpkin, eggs, orange juice and vanilla until well blended. (Mixture may appear curdled.) Add to flour mixture; stir until just moistened. Spoon evenly into prepared muffin cups, filling each cup ¾ full.

2. Bake 12 to 15 minutes or until toothpick inserted into centers comes out clean. Remove muffins from pans. Place cinnamon sugar in small bowl. Roll warm muffins in sugar. Serve immediately. *Makes 36 miniature-size or 12 regular-size muffins*

Pumpkin Spice Mini Muffins

1 jar Pumpkin Spice Mini Muffin Mix
½ cup (1 stick) butter, softened
1 cup solid pack pumpkin
2 eggs
½ cup orange juice
1 teaspoon vanilla

1. Preheat oven to 400°F. Grease or paper line 36 mini (1¾-inch) or 12 regular-size (2½-inch) muffin cups. Remove cinnamon sugar packet from jar. Place contents of jar in large bowl; stir until well blended. Beat butter in medium bowl with electric mixer on medium speed until creamy. Beat in pumpkin, eggs, orange juice and vanilla until well blended. (Mixture may appear curdled.) Add to flour mixture; stir until just moistened. Spoon evenly into prepared muffin cups, filling each cup ¾ full.

2. Bake 12 to 15 minutes or until toothpick inserted into centers comes out clean. Remove muffins from pans. Place cinnamon sugar in small bowl. Roll warm muffins in sugar. Serve immediately. *Makes 36 miniature-size or 12 regular-size muffins*

Luscious Orange Cranberry Scone Mix

- 1 cup all-purpose flour
- ¾ cup dried cranberries or dried blueberries
- ½ cup packed brown sugar
- ¼ cup granulated sugar
- 1 cup all-purpose flour
- 2 teaspoons baking powder
- ½ teaspoon ground ginger
- ½ teaspoon ground cinnamon
- ¼ teaspoon baking soda
- ¼ teaspoon salt
- ½ cup powdered sugar

Layer all ingredients except powdered sugar in the order listed above in 1-quart food storage jar with tight-fitting lid. Lightly pack down ingredients before adding another layer. Place powdered sugar in small plastic food storage bag. Close with twist tie; cut off top of bag. Place bag in jar. Cover top of jar with fabric; attach gift tag with raffia or ribbon. *Makes 1 (1-quart) jar*

Lemon Blueberry Scones: Substitute dried blueberries for cranberries in the jar mix. Substitute lemon flavors when preparing scones.

Luscious Orange Cranberry Scones

- **1 jar Luscious Orange Cranberry Scone Mix**
- **6 tablespoons (¾ stick) butter, cut into pieces and softened**
- **½ cup buttermilk**
- **1 egg**
- **2 teaspoons grated orange or lemon peel**
- **1 teaspoon orange or lemon extract**
- **2 to 3 teaspoons orange or lemon juice**

Preheat oven to 350°F. Grease baking sheets. Remove powdered sugar packet from jar. Place remaining contents of jar into bowl. Cut in butter with pastry blender until mixture resembles coarse crumbs. Whisk together buttermilk, egg, orange peel and orange extract. Pour buttermilk mixture into flour mixture. Stir until stiff dough is formed. Knead in bowl. Drop by ¼ cupfuls onto prepared baking sheets. Bake 18 to 20 minutes or until toothpick inserted into centers comes out clean. Remove to wire racks. Stir together powdered sugar and orange juice to make glaze. Drizzle over scones. Serve warm.

Makes 12 scones

Lemon Blueberry Scones: If jar mix contains dried blueberries, prepare scones with lemon flavors.

Luscious Orange Cranberry Scones

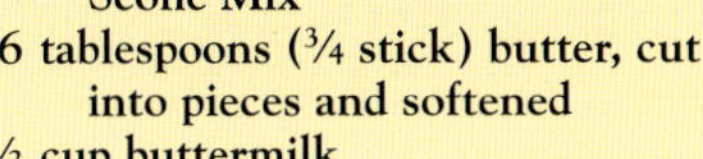

1 jar Luscious Orange Cranberry Scone Mix
6 tablespoons (¾ stick) butter, cut into pieces and softened
½ cup buttermilk
1 egg
2 teaspoons grated orange or lemon peel
1 teaspoon orange or lemon extract
2 to 3 teaspoons orange or lemon juice

Preheat oven to 350°F. Grease baking sheets. Remove powdered sugar packet from jar. Place remaining contents of jar into bowl. Cut in butter with pastry blender until mixture resembles coarse crumbs. Whisk together buttermilk, egg, orange peel and orange extract. Pour buttermilk mixture into flour mixture. Stir until stiff dough is formed. Knead in bowl. Drop by ¼ cupfuls onto prepared baking sheets. Bake 18 to 20 minutes or until toothpick inserted into centers comes out clean. Remove to wire racks. Stir together powdered sugar and orange juice to make glaze. Drizzle over scones. Serve warm. *Makes 12 scones*

Lemon Blueberry Scones: If jar mix contains dried blueberries, prepare scones with lemon flavors.

Luscious Orange Cranberry Scones

1 jar Luscious Orange Cranberry Scone Mix
6 tablespoons (¾ stick) butter, cut into pieces and softened
½ cup buttermilk
1 egg
2 teaspoons grated orange or lemon peel
1 teaspoon orange or lemon extract
2 to 3 teaspoons orange or lemon juice

Preheat oven to 350°F. Grease baking sheets. Remove powdered sugar packet from jar. Place remaining contents of jar into bowl. Cut in butter with pastry blender until mixture resembles coarse crumbs. Whisk together buttermilk, egg, orange peel and orange extract. Pour buttermilk mixture into flour mixture. Stir until stiff dough is formed. Knead in bowl. Drop by ¼ cupfuls onto prepared baking sheets. Bake 18 to 20 minutes or until toothpick inserted into centers comes out clean. Remove to wire racks. Stir together powdered sugar and orange juice to make glaze. Drizzle over scones. Serve warm. *Makes 12 scones*

Lemon Blueberry Scones: If jar mix contains dried blueberries, prepare scones with lemon flavors.

Luscious Orange Cranberry Scones

1 jar Luscious Orange Cranberry Scone Mix
6 tablespoons (¾ stick) butter, cut into pieces and softened
½ cup buttermilk
1 egg
2 teaspoons grated orange or lemon peel
1 teaspoon orange or lemon extract
2 to 3 teaspoons orange or lemon juice

Preheat oven to 350°F. Grease baking sheets. Remove powdered sugar packet from jar. Place remaining contents of jar into bowl. Cut in butter with pastry blender until mixture resembles coarse crumbs. Whisk together buttermilk, egg, orange peel and orange extract. Pour buttermilk mixture into flour mixture. Stir until stiff dough is formed. Knead in bowl. Drop by ¼ cupfuls onto prepared baking sheets. Bake 18 to 20 minutes or until toothpick inserted into centers comes out clean. Remove to wire racks. Stir together powdered sugar and orange juice to make glaze. Drizzle over scones. Serve warm. *Makes 12 scones*

Lemon Blueberry Scones: If jar mix contains dried blueberries, prepare scones with lemon flavors.

Luscious Orange Cranberry Scones

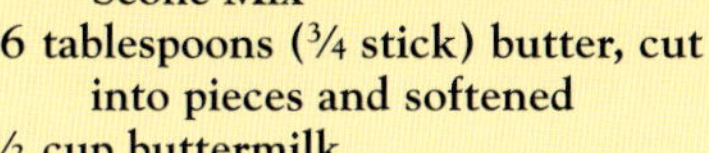

1 jar Luscious Orange Cranberry Scone Mix
6 tablespoons (¾ stick) butter, cut into pieces and softened
½ cup buttermilk
1 egg
2 teaspoons grated orange or lemon peel
1 teaspoon orange or lemon extract
2 to 3 teaspoons orange or lemon juice

Preheat oven to 350°F. Grease baking sheets. Remove powdered sugar packet from jar. Place remaining contents of jar into bowl. Cut in butter with pastry blender until mixture resembles coarse crumbs. Whisk together buttermilk, egg, orange peel and orange extract. Pour buttermilk mixture into flour mixture. Stir until stiff dough is formed. Knead in bowl. Drop by ¼ cupfuls onto prepared baking sheets. Bake 18 to 20 minutes or until toothpick inserted into centers comes out clean. Remove to wire racks. Stir together powdered sugar and orange juice to make glaze. Drizzle over scones. Serve warm. *Makes 12 scones*

Lemon Blueberry Scones: If jar mix contains dried blueberries, prepare scones with lemon flavors.

Luscious Orange Cranberry Scones

1 jar Luscious Orange Cranberry Scone Mix
6 tablespoons (¾ stick) butter, cut into pieces and softened
½ cup buttermilk
1 egg
2 teaspoons grated orange or lemon peel
1 teaspoon orange or lemon extract
2 to 3 teaspoons orange or lemon juice

Preheat oven to 350°F. Grease baking sheets. Remove powdered sugar packet from jar. Place remaining contents of jar into bowl. Cut in butter with pastry blender until mixture resembles coarse crumbs. Whisk together buttermilk, egg, orange peel and orange extract. Pour buttermilk mixture into flour mixture. Stir until stiff dough is formed. Knead in bowl. Drop by ¼ cupfuls onto prepared baking sheets. Bake 18 to 20 minutes or until toothpick inserted into centers comes out clean. Remove to wire racks. Stir together powdered sugar and orange juice to make glaze. Drizzle over scones. Serve warm. *Makes 12 scones*

Lemon Blueberry Scones: If jar mix contains dried blueberries, prepare scones with lemon flavors.

Luscious Orange Cranberry Scones

1 jar Luscious Orange Cranberry Scone Mix
6 tablespoons (¾ stick) butter, cut into pieces and softened
½ cup buttermilk
1 egg
2 teaspoons grated orange or lemon peel
1 teaspoon orange or lemon extract
2 to 3 teaspoons orange or lemon juice

Preheat oven to 350°F. Grease baking sheets. Remove powdered sugar packet from jar. Place remaining contents of jar into bowl. Cut in butter with pastry blender until mixture resembles coarse crumbs. Whisk together buttermilk, egg, orange peel and orange extract. Pour buttermilk mixture into flour mixture. Stir until stiff dough is formed. Knead in bowl. Drop by ¼ cupfuls onto prepared baking sheets. Bake 18 to 20 minutes or until toothpick inserted into centers comes out clean. Remove to wire racks. Stir together powdered sugar and orange juice to make glaze. Drizzle over scones. Serve warm. *Makes 12 scones*

Lemon Blueberry Scones: If jar mix contains dried blueberries, prepare scones with lemon flavors.

Eggnog Cherry Quick Bread Mix

1 cup all-purpose flour
¾ cup sugar
½ cup chopped candied or dried cherries
¾ cup chopped pecans
1¼ cups all-purpose flour
1 tablespoon baking powder
1 teaspoon ground nutmeg
½ teaspoon salt

1. Layer all ingredients in the order listed above in 1-quart food storage jar with tight-fitting lid. Lightly pack down ingredients before adding another layer.

2. Cover top of jar with fabric; attach gift tag with raffia or ribbon.

Makes 1 (1-quart) jar

Eggnog Cherry Quick Bread

- **1 jar Eggnog Cherry Quick Bread Mix**
- **1¼ cups prepared dairy eggnog or half-and-half**
- **2 eggs**
- **6 tablespoons (¾ stick) butter, melted and cooled**
- **1 teaspoon vanilla**

1. Preheat oven to 350°F. Spray 3 miniature (5½×3-inch) loaf pans with nonstick cooking spray.
2. Place contents of jar into large bowl; stir until blended. Whisk together eggnog, eggs, butter and vanilla in separate bowl. Add eggnog mixture to flour mixture; stir until just moistened. Divide evenly among prepared pans.
3. Bake 35 to 40 minutes or until toothpick inserted into centers comes out clean. Cool in pans 15 minutes. Remove to wire racks; cool completely. Store tightly wrapped in plastic wrap at room temperature.

Makes 3 miniature loaves

Eggnog Cherry Quick Bread

1 jar Eggnog Cherry Quick Bread Mix
1¼ cups prepared dairy eggnog or half-and-half
2 eggs
6 tablespoons (¾ stick) butter, melted and cooled
1 teaspoon vanilla

1. Preheat oven to 350°F. Spray 3 miniature (5½×3-inch) loaf pans with nonstick cooking spray.

2. Place contents of jar into large bowl; stir until blended. Whisk together eggnog, eggs, butter and vanilla in separate bowl. Add eggnog mixture to flour mixture; stir until just moistened. Divide evenly among prepared pans.

3. Bake 35 to 40 minutes or until toothpick inserted into centers comes out clean. Cool in pans 15 minutes. Remove to wire racks; cool completely. Store tightly wrapped in plastic wrap at room temperature. *Makes 3 miniature loaves*

Eggnog Cherry Quick Bread

1 jar Eggnog Cherry Quick Bread Mix
1¼ cups prepared dairy eggnog or half-and-half
2 eggs
6 tablespoons (¾ stick) butter, melted and cooled
1 teaspoon vanilla

1. Preheat oven to 350°F. Spray 3 miniature (5½×3-inch) loaf pans with nonstick cooking spray.

2. Place contents of jar into large bowl; stir until blended. Whisk together eggnog, eggs, butter and vanilla in separate bowl. Add eggnog mixture to flour mixture; stir until just moistened. Divide evenly among prepared pans.

3. Bake 35 to 40 minutes or until toothpick inserted into centers comes out clean. Cool in pans 15 minutes. Remove to wire racks; cool completely. Store tightly wrapped in plastic wrap at room temperature. *Makes 3 miniature loaves*

Eggnog Cherry Quick Bread

1 jar Eggnog Cherry Quick Bread Mix
1¼ cups prepared dairy eggnog or half-and-half
2 eggs
6 tablespoons (¾ stick) butter, melted and cooled
1 teaspoon vanilla

1. Preheat oven to 350°F. Spray 3 miniature (5½×3-inch) loaf pans with nonstick cooking spray.

2. Place contents of jar into large bowl; stir until blended. Whisk together eggnog, eggs, butter and vanilla in separate bowl. Add eggnog mixture to flour mixture; stir until just moistened. Divide evenly among prepared pans.

3. Bake 35 to 40 minutes or until toothpick inserted into centers comes out clean. Cool in pans 15 minutes. Remove to wire racks; cool completely. Store tightly wrapped in plastic wrap at room temperature. *Makes 3 miniature loaves*

Eggnog Cherry Quick Bread

1 jar Eggnog Cherry Quick Bread Mix
1¼ cups prepared dairy eggnog or half-and-half
2 eggs
6 tablespoons (¾ stick) butter, melted and cooled
1 teaspoon vanilla

1. Preheat oven to 350°F. Spray 3 miniature (5½×3-inch) loaf pans with nonstick cooking spray.

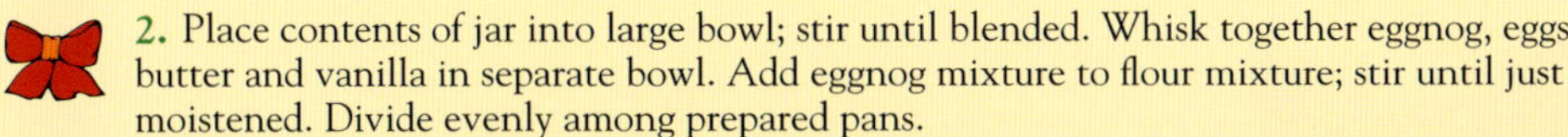

2. Place contents of jar into large bowl; stir until blended. Whisk together eggnog, eggs, butter and vanilla in separate bowl. Add eggnog mixture to flour mixture; stir until just moistened. Divide evenly among prepared pans.

3. Bake 35 to 40 minutes or until toothpick inserted into centers comes out clean. Cool in pans 15 minutes. Remove to wire racks; cool completely. Store tightly wrapped in plastic wrap at room temperature.

Makes 3 miniature loaves

Eggnog Cherry Quick Bread

1 jar Eggnog Cherry Quick Bread Mix
1¼ cups prepared dairy eggnog or half-and-half
2 eggs
6 tablespoons (¾ stick) butter, melted and cooled
1 teaspoon vanilla

1. Preheat oven to 350°F. Spray 3 miniature (5½×3-inch) loaf pans with nonstick cooking spray.

2. Place contents of jar into large bowl; stir until blended. Whisk together eggnog, eggs, butter and vanilla in separate bowl. Add eggnog mixture to flour mixture; stir until just moistened. Divide evenly among prepared pans.

3. Bake 35 to 40 minutes or until toothpick inserted into centers comes out clean. Cool in pans 15 minutes. Remove to wire racks; cool completely. Store tightly wrapped in plastic wrap at room temperature.

Makes 3 miniature loaves

Eggnog Cherry Quick Bread

1 jar Eggnog Cherry Quick Bread Mix
1¼ cups prepared dairy eggnog or half-and-half
2 eggs
6 tablespoons (¾ stick) butter, melted and cooled
1 teaspoon vanilla

1. Preheat oven to 350°F. Spray 3 miniature (5½×3-inch) loaf pans with nonstick cooking spray.

2. Place contents of jar into large bowl; stir until blended. Whisk together eggnog, eggs, butter and vanilla in separate bowl. Add eggnog mixture to flour mixture; stir until just moistened. Divide evenly among prepared pans.

3. Bake 35 to 40 minutes or until toothpick inserted into centers comes out clean. Cool in pans 15 minutes. Remove to wire racks; cool completely. Store tightly wrapped in plastic wrap at room temperature.

Makes 3 miniature loaves

Elegant Pecan Brandy Cake Mix

1¼ cups all-purpose flour
¾ cup packed brown sugar
1¼ cups granulated sugar
½ cup cornmeal
1 cup all-purpose flour
2 teaspoons baking powder
½ teaspoon salt
1 teaspoon ground cinnamon
¼ teaspoon ground nutmeg
1 cup coarsely chopped pecans, toasted*
1 cup powdered sugar

*Place nuts in a microwavable dish. Microwave on HIGH 1 to 2 minutes or just until light golden brown, stirring nuts every 30 seconds. Allow to stand 3 minutes. Cool completely.

1. Layer all ingredients except powdered sugar in the order listed above in 2-quart food storage jar with tight-fitting lid. Place powdered sugar in small plastic food storage bag. Close with twist tie; cut off top of bag. Place bag in jar.
2. Cover top of jar with fabric; attach gift tag with raffia or ribbon.

Makes 1 (2-quart) jar

Elegant Pecan Brandy Cake

1 jar Elegant Pecan Brandy Cake Mix
1 cup (2 sticks) plus 2 tablespoons butter, softened
1 cup sour cream
5 eggs
½ cup plus 1 teaspoon brandy or rum
1 teaspoon vanilla
4 to 5 teaspoons milk

Preheat oven to 325°F. Generously grease and flour 10-inch Bundt pan. Remove powdered sugar packet from jar. Pour contents of jar into bowl; stir until well blended. Beat 1 cup butter and sour cream in separate bowl with electric mixer on medium speed until smooth. Beat in eggs, one at a time. Add ½ cup brandy and vanilla. Gradually add flour mixture, beating until blended. Spread into prepared pan. Bake 50 to 65 minutes or until toothpick inserted near center comes out clean. Cool cake 10 minutes in pan on wire rack. Loosen edges; remove cake to wire rack. Heat remaining 2 tablespoons butter in saucepan over medium heat until melted and golden brown; cool slightly. Add powdered sugar, remaining 1 teaspoon brandy and enough milk to make glaze; stir until smooth. Drizzle over cake. *Makes 1 (10-inch) cake*

Elegant Pecan Brandy Cake

- 1 jar Elegant Pecan Brandy Cake Mix
- 1 cup (2 sticks) plus 2 tablespoons butter, softened, divided
- 1 cup sour cream
- 5 eggs
- ½ cup plus 1 teaspoon brandy or rum
- 1 teaspoon vanilla
- 4 to 5 teaspoons milk

Preheat oven to 325°F. Generously grease and flour 10-inch Bundt pan. Remove powdered sugar packet from jar. Pour contents of jar into bowl; stir until well blended. Beat 1 cup butter and sour cream in separate bowl with electric mixer on medium speed until smooth. Beat in eggs, one at a time. Add ½ cup brandy and vanilla. Gradually add flour mixture, beating until blended. Spread into prepared pan. Bake 50 to 65 minutes or until toothpick inserted near center comes out clean. Cool cake 10 minutes in pan on wire rack. Loosen edges; remove cake to wire rack. Heat remaining 2 tablespoons butter in saucepan over medium heat until melted and golden brown; cool slightly. Add powdered sugar, remaining 1 teaspoon brandy and enough milk to make glaze; stir until smooth. Drizzle over cake.

Makes 1 (10-inch) cake

Elegant Pecan Brandy Cake

- 1 jar Elegant Pecan Brandy Cake Mix
- 1 cup (2 sticks) plus 2 tablespoons butter, softened, divided
- 1 cup sour cream
- 5 eggs
- ½ cup plus 1 teaspoon brandy or rum
- 1 teaspoon vanilla
- 4 to 5 teaspoons milk

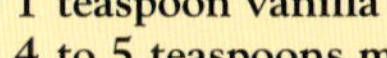

Preheat oven to 325°F. Generously grease and flour 10-inch Bundt pan. Remove powdered sugar packet from jar. Pour contents of jar into bowl; stir until well blended. Beat 1 cup butter and sour cream in separate bowl with electric mixer on medium speed until smooth. Beat in eggs, one at a time. Add ½ cup brandy and vanilla. Gradually add flour mixture, beating until blended. Spread into prepared pan. Bake 50 to 65 minutes or until toothpick inserted near center comes out clean. Cool cake 10 minutes in pan on wire rack. Loosen edges; remove cake to wire rack. Heat remaining 2 tablespoons butter in saucepan over medium heat until melted and golden brown; cool slightly. Add powdered sugar, remaining 1 teaspoon brandy and enough milk to make glaze; stir until smooth. Drizzle over cake.

Makes 1 (10-inch) cake

Elegant Pecan Brandy Cake

- 1 jar Elegant Pecan Brandy Cake Mix
- 1 cup (2 sticks) plus 2 tablespoons butter, softened, divided
- 1 cup sour cream
- 5 eggs
- ½ cup plus 1 teaspoon brandy or rum
- 1 teaspoon vanilla
- 4 to 5 teaspoons milk

Preheat oven to 325°F. Generously grease and flour 10-inch Bundt pan. Remove powdered sugar packet from jar. Pour contents of jar into bowl; stir until well blended. Beat 1 cup butter and sour cream in separate bowl with electric mixer on medium speed until smooth. Beat in eggs, one at a time. Add ½ cup brandy and vanilla. Gradually add flour mixture, beating until blended. Spread into prepared pan. Bake 50 to 65 minutes or until toothpick inserted near center comes out clean. Cool cake 10 minutes in pan on wire rack. Loosen edges; remove cake to wire rack. Heat remaining 2 tablespoons butter in saucepan over medium heat until melted and golden brown; cool slightly. Add powdered sugar, remaining 1 teaspoon brandy and enough milk to make glaze; stir until smooth. Drizzle over cake.

Makes 1 (10-inch) cake

Elegant Pecan Brandy Cake

1 jar Elegant Pecan Brandy Cake Mix
1 cup (2 sticks) plus 2 tablespoons butter, softened, divided
1 cup sour cream
5 eggs
½ cup plus 1 teaspoon brandy or rum
1 teaspoon vanilla
4 to 5 teaspoons milk

Preheat oven to 325°F. Generously grease and flour 10-inch Bundt pan. Remove powdered sugar packet from jar. Pour contents of jar into bowl; stir until well blended. Beat 1 cup butter and sour cream in separate bowl with electric mixer on medium speed until smooth. Beat in eggs, one at a time. Add ½ cup brandy and vanilla. Gradually add flour mixture, beating until blended. Spread into prepared pan. Bake 50 to 65 minutes or until toothpick inserted near center comes out clean. Cool cake 10 minutes in pan on wire rack. Loosen edges; remove cake to wire rack. Heat remaining 2 tablespoons butter in saucepan over medium heat until melted and golden brown; cool slightly. Add powdered sugar, remaining 1 teaspoon brandy and enough milk to make glaze; stir until smooth. Drizzle over cake.

Makes 1 (10-inch) cake

Elegant Pecan Brandy Cake

1 jar Elegant Pecan Brandy Cake Mix
1 cup (2 sticks) plus 2 tablespoons butter, softened, divided
1 cup sour cream
5 eggs
½ cup plus 1 teaspoon brandy or rum
1 teaspoon vanilla
4 to 5 teaspoons milk

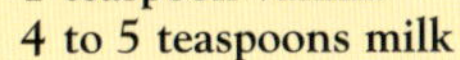

Preheat oven to 325°F. Generously grease and flour 10-inch Bundt pan. Remove powdered sugar packet from jar. Pour contents of jar into bowl; stir until well blended. Beat 1 cup butter and sour cream in separate bowl with electric mixer on medium speed until smooth. Beat in eggs, one at a time. Add ½ cup brandy and vanilla. Gradually add flour mixture, beating until blended. Spread into prepared pan. Bake 50 to 65 minutes or until toothpick inserted near center comes out clean. Cool cake 10 minutes in pan on wire rack. Loosen edges; remove cake to wire rack. Heat remaining 2 tablespoons butter in saucepan over medium heat until melted and golden brown; cool slightly. Add powdered sugar, remaining 1 teaspoon brandy and enough milk to make glaze; stir until smooth. Drizzle over cake.

Makes 1 (10-inch) cake

Elegant Pecan Brandy Cake

1 jar Elegant Pecan Brandy Cake Mix
1 cup (2 sticks) plus 2 tablespoons butter, softened, divided
1 cup sour cream
5 eggs
½ cup plus 1 teaspoon brandy or rum
1 teaspoon vanilla
4 to 5 teaspoons milk

Preheat oven to 325°F. Generously grease and flour 10-inch Bundt pan. Remove powdered sugar packet from jar. Pour contents of jar into bowl; stir until well blended. Beat 1 cup butter and sour cream in separate bowl with electric mixer on medium speed until smooth. Beat in eggs, one at a time. Add ½ cup brandy and vanilla. Gradually add flour mixture, beating until blended. Spread into prepared pan. Bake 50 to 65 minutes or until toothpick inserted near center comes out clean. Cool cake 10 minutes in pan on wire rack. Loosen edges; remove cake to wire rack. Heat remaining 2 tablespoons butter in saucepan over medium heat until melted and golden brown; cool slightly. Add powdered sugar, remaining 1 teaspoon brandy and enough milk to make glaze; stir until smooth. Drizzle over cake.

Makes 1 (10-inch) cake

Mistletoe Kiss Me Cake Mix

1 cup sugar
1 cup all-purpose flour
1 teaspoon baking soda
1 teaspoon salt
1 teaspoon dried orange peel
½ teaspoon ground nutmeg
⅓ cup chopped walnuts
1 cup raisins, coarsely chopped
1 cup all-purpose flour
¼ cup sugar
1 teaspoon ground cinnamon

1. Layer all ingredients except ¼ cup sugar and cinnamon in the order listed above in wide-mouth 1-quart food storage jar with tight-fitting lid. Place sugar and cinnamon in small plastic food storage bag. Close with twist tie; cut off top of bag. Place bag in jar.
2. Cover top of jar with fabric; attach gift tag with raffia or ribbon.

Makes 1 (1-quart) jar

Mistletoe Kiss Me Cakes

1 jar Mistletoe Kiss Me Cake Mix
½ cup (1 stick) butter, softened
2 eggs
½ cup milk
¾ cup orange juice, divided
2 teaspoons grated orange peel

1. Preheat oven to 350°F. Grease and flour 6 (4-inch) miniature Bundt pans.

2. Remove cinnamon sugar packet from jar. Pour remaining contents of jar into medium bowl; stir until well blended. Beat butter in large bowl with electric mixer on medium speed until smooth. Beat in eggs, one at a time. Add milk, ½ cup orange juice and orange peel; beat until well blended. Gradually add flour mixture, beating until blended. Divide evenly among prepared pans.

3. Bake 20 to 25 minutes or until toothpick inserted near centers comes out clean. Cool in pans 10 minutes. Loosen edges; remove to wire rack. Cool completely. Pour remaining ¼ cup juice over cakes. Sprinkle with cinnamon sugar. *Makes 6 miniature cakes*

Mistletoe Kiss Me Cakes

- **1 jar Mistletoe Kiss Me Cake Mix**
- **½ cup (1 stick) butter, softened**
- **2 eggs**
- **½ cup milk**
- **¾ cup orange juice, divided**
- **2 teaspoons grated orange peel**

1. Preheat oven to 350°F. Grease and flour 6 (4-inch) miniature Bundt pans.

2. Remove cinnamon sugar packet from jar. Pour remaining contents of jar into medium bowl; stir until well blended. Beat butter in large bowl with electric mixer on medium speed until smoothh. Beat in eggs, one at a time. Add milk, ½ cup orange juice and orange peel; beat until well blended. Gradually add flour mixture, beating until blended. Divide evenly among prepared pans.

3. Bake 20 to 25 minutes or until toothpick inserted near centers comes out clean. Cool in pans 10 minutes. Loosen edges; remove to wire rack. Cool completely. Pour remaining ¼ cup juice over cakes. Sprinkle with cinnamon sugar.

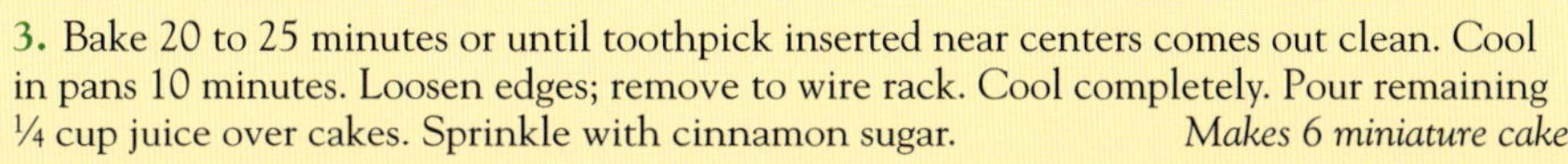

Makes 6 miniature cakes

Mistletoe Kiss Me Cakes

- **1 jar Mistletoe Kiss Me Cake Mix**
- **½ cup (1 stick) butter, softened**
- **2 eggs**
- **½ cup milk**
- **¾ cup orange juice, divided**
- **2 teaspoons grated orange peel**

1. Preheat oven to 350°F. Grease and flour 6 (4-inch) miniature Bundt pans.

2. Remove cinnamon sugar packet from jar. Pour remaining contents of jar into medium bowl; stir until well blended. Beat butter in large bowl with electric mixer on medium speed until smooth. Beat in eggs, one at a time. Add milk, ½ cup orange juice and orange peel; beat until well blended. Gradually add flour mixture, beating until blended. Divide evenly among prepared pans.

3. Bake 20 to 25 minutes or until toothpick inserted near centers comes out clean. Cool in pans 10 minutes. Loosen edges; remove to wire rack. Cool completely. Pour remaining ¼ cup juice over cakes. Sprinkle with cinnamon sugar.

Makes 6 miniature cakes

Mistletoe Kiss Me Cakes

- **1 jar Mistletoe Kiss Me Cake Mix**
- **½ cup (1 stick) butter, softened**
- **2 eggs**
- **½ cup milk**
- **¾ cup orange juice, divided**
- **2 teaspoons grated orange peel**

1. Preheat oven to 350°F. Grease and flour 6 (4-inch) miniature Bundt pans.

2. Remove cinnamon sugar packet from jar. Pour remaining contents of jar into medium bowl; stir until well blended. Beat butter in large bowl with electric mixer on medium speed until smooth. Beat in eggs, one at a time. Add milk, ½ cup orange juice and orange peel; beat until well blended. Gradually add flour mixture, beating until blended. Divide evenly among prepared pans.

3. Bake 20 to 25 minutes or until toothpick inserted near centers comes out clean. Cool in pans 10 minutes. Loosen edges; remove to wire rack. Cool completely. Pour remaining ¼ cup juice over cakes. Sprinkle with cinnamon sugar.

Makes 6 miniature cakes

Mistletoe Kiss Me Cakes

1 jar Mistletoe Kiss Me Cake Mix
½ cup (1 stick) butter, softened
2 eggs
½ cup milk
¾ cup orange juice, divided
2 teaspoons grated orange peel

1. Preheat oven to 350°F. Grease and flour 6 (4-inch) miniature Bundt pans.

2. Remove cinnamon sugar packet from jar. Pour remaining contents of jar into medium bowl; stir until well blended. Beat butter in large bowl with electric mixer on medium speed until smooth. Beat in eggs, one at a time. Add milk, ½ cup orange juice and orange peel; beat until well blended. Gradually add flour mixture, beating until blended. Divide evenly among prepared pans.

3. Bake 20 to 25 minutes or until toothpick inserted near centers comes out clean. Cool in pans 10 minutes. Loosen edges; remove to wire rack. Cool completely. Pour remaining ¼ cup juice over cakes. Sprinkle with cinnamon sugar. *Makes 6 miniature cakes*

Mistletoe Kiss Me Cakes

1 jar Mistletoe Kiss Me Cake Mix
½ cup (1 stick) butter, softened
2 eggs
½ cup milk
¾ cup orange juice, divided
2 teaspoons grated orange peel

1. Preheat oven to 350°F. Grease and flour 6 (4-inch) miniature Bundt pans.

2. Remove cinnamon sugar packet from jar. Pour remaining contents of jar into medium bowl; stir until well blended. Beat butter in large bowl with electric mixer on medium speed until smooth. Beat in eggs, one at a time. Add milk, ½ cup orange juice and orange peel; beat until well blended. Gradually add flour mixture, beating until blended. Divide evenly among prepared pans.

3. Bake 20 to 25 minutes or until toothpick inserted near centers comes out clean. Cool in pans 10 minutes. Loosen edges; remove to wire rack. Cool completely. Pour remaining ¼ cup juice over cakes. Sprinkle with cinnamon sugar. *Makes 6 miniature cakes*

Mistletoe Kiss Me Cakes

1 jar Mistletoe Kiss Me Cake Mix
½ cup (1 stick) butter, softened
2 eggs
½ cup milk
¾ cup orange juice, divided
2 teaspoons grated orange peel

1. Preheat oven to 350°F. Grease and flour 6 (4-inch) miniature Bundt pans.

2. Remove cinnamon sugar packet from jar. Pour remaining contents of jar into medium bowl; stir until well blended. Beat butter in large bowl with electric mixer on medium speed until smooth. Beat in eggs, one at a time. Add milk, ½ cup orange juice and orange peel; beat until well blended. Gradually add flour mixture, beating until blended. Divide evenly among prepared pans.

3. Bake 20 to 25 minutes or until toothpick inserted near centers comes out clean. Cool in pans 10 minutes. Loosen edges; remove to wire rack. Cool completely. Pour remaining ¼ cup juice over cakes. Sprinkle with cinnamon sugar. *Makes 6 miniature cakes*

Cherry Pistachio Biscotti Mix

1½ cups all-purpose flour
1¼ teaspoons baking powder
½ teaspoon salt
½ teaspoon ground ginger
½ teaspoon ground cinnamon
½ cup dried tart cherries or chopped apricots
½ cup packed brown sugar
¼ cup granulated sugar
½ cup pistachios or almonds, toasted*
2 tablespoons raw (turbinado) sugar

*To toast nuts, spread in single layer on baking sheet. Bake in preheated 350°F oven 8 to 10 minutes or until golden brown, stirring frequently.

1. Layer all ingredients except raw sugar in the order listed above in 1-quart food storage jar with tight-fitting lid. Place raw sugar in small plastic food storage bag. Close with twist tie; cut off top of bag. Place bag in jar.

2. Cover top of jar with fabric; attach gift tag with raffia or ribbon.

Makes 1 (1-quart) jar

Cherry Pistachio Biscotti

- **1 jar Cherry Pistachio Biscotti Mix**
- **5 tablespoons butter, cut into pieces**
- **1 egg**
- **2 tablespoons milk or almond-flavored liqueur**
- **1 teaspoon almond extract or vanilla**

1. Preheat oven to 350°F. Lightly grease cookie sheet. Remove sugar packet from jar. Place remaining contents of jar in large bowl; stir until well blended. Cut in butter with pastry blender or two knives until mixture resembles coarse crumbs. Whisk together egg, milk and almond extract in small bowl. Add to flour mixture, stirring to form stiff dough. Knead dough in bowl. Divide dough in half; shape into two 9×2-inch logs. Place 2 inches apart on prepared cookie sheet. Sprinkle sugar over each log.

2. Bake 25 minutes or until logs are lightly browned. Cool logs on wire rack 15 minutes. *Reduce heat to 325°F.* Slice each log diagonally into ¾-inch-thick slices. Place slices, cut side up, on cookie sheet. Bake 10 minutes; turn biscotti over. Bake 5 to 10 minutes or until surfaces are golden brown and cookies are dry. Remove biscotti to wire racks; cool completely.

Makes about 1½ dozen biscotti

Cherry Pistachio Biscotti

1 jar Cherry Pistachio Biscotti Mix
5 tablespoons butter, cut into pieces
1 egg
2 tablespoons milk or almond-flavored liqueur
1 teaspoon almond extract or vanilla

1. Preheat oven to 350°F. Lightly grease cookie sheet. Remove sugar packet from jar. Place remaining contents of jar in large bowl; stir until well blended. Cut in butter with pastry blender or two knives until mixture resembles coarse crumbs. Whisk together egg, milk and almond extract in small bowl. Add to flour mixture, stirring to form stiff dough. Knead dough in bowl. Divide dough in half; shape into two 9×2-inch logs. Place 2 inches apart on prepared cookie sheet. Sprinkle sugar over each log.

2. Bake 25 minutes or until logs are lightly browned. Cool logs on wire rack 15 minutes. *Reduce heat to 325°F.* Slice each log diagonally into ¾-inch-thick slices. Place slices, cut side up, on cookie sheet. Bake 10 minutes; turn biscotti over. Bake 5 to 10 minutes or until surfaces are golden brown and cookies are dry. Remove biscotti to wire racks; cool completely.

Makes about 1½ dozen biscotti

Cherry Pistachio Biscotti

1 jar Cherry Pistachio Biscotti Mix
5 tablespoons butter, cut into pieces
1 egg
2 tablespoons milk or almond-flavored liqueur
1 teaspoon almond extract or vanilla

1. Preheat oven to 350°F. Lightly grease cookie sheet. Remove sugar packet from jar. Place remaining contents of jar in large bowl; stir until well blended. Cut in butter with pastry blender or two knives until mixture resembles coarse crumbs. Whisk together egg, milk and almond extract in small bowl. Add to flour mixture, stirring to form stiff dough. Knead dough in bowl. Divide dough in half; shape into two 9×2-inch logs. Place 2 inches apart on prepared cookie sheet. Sprinkle sugar over each log.

2. Bake 25 minutes or until logs are lightly browned. Cool logs on wire rack 15 minutes. *Reduce heat to 325°F.* Slice each log diagonally into ¾-inch-thick slices. Place slices, cut side up, on cookie sheet. Bake 10 minutes; turn biscotti over. Bake 5 to 10 minutes or until surfaces are golden brown and cookies are dry. Remove biscotti to wire racks; cool completely.

Makes about 1½ dozen biscotti

Cherry Pistachio Biscotti

1 jar Cherry Pistachio Biscotti Mix
5 tablespoons butter, cut into pieces
1 egg
2 tablespoons milk or almond-flavored liqueur
1 teaspoon almond extract or vanilla

1. Preheat oven to 350°F. Lightly grease cookie sheet. Remove sugar packet from jar. Place remaining contents of jar in large bowl; stir until well blended. Cut in butter with pastry blender or two knives until mixture resembles coarse crumbs. Whisk together egg, milk and almond extract in small bowl. Add to flour mixture, stirring to form stiff dough. Knead dough in bowl. Divide dough in half; shape into two 9×2-inch logs. Place 2 inches apart on prepared cookie sheet. Sprinkle sugar over each log.

2. Bake 25 minutes or until logs are lightly browned. Cool logs on wire rack 15 minutes. *Reduce heat to 325°F.* Slice each log diagonally into ¾-inch-thick slices. Place slices, cut side up, on cookie sheet. Bake 10 minutes; turn biscotti over. Bake 5 to 10 minutes or until surfaces are golden brown and cookies are dry. Remove biscotti to wire racks; cool completely.

Makes about 1½ dozen biscotti

Cherry Pistachio Biscotti

- 1 jar Cherry Pistachio Biscotti Mix
- 5 tablespoons butter, cut into pieces
- 1 egg
- 2 tablespoons milk or almond-flavored liqueur
- 1 teaspoon almond extract or vanilla

1. Preheat oven to 350°F. Lightly grease cookie sheet. Remove sugar packet from jar. Place remaining contents of jar in large bowl; stir until well blended. Cut in butter with pastry blender or two knives until mixture resembles coarse crumbs. Whisk together egg, milk and almond extract in small bowl. Add to flour mixture, stirring to form stiff dough. Knead dough in bowl. Divide dough in half; shape into two 9×2-inch logs. Place 2 inches apart on prepared cookie sheet. Sprinkle sugar over each log.

2. Bake 25 minutes or until logs are lightly browned. Cool logs on wire rack 15 minutes. *Reduce heat to 325°F.* Slice each log diagonally into ¾-inch-thick slices. Place slices, cut side up, on cookie sheet. Bake 10 minutes; turn biscotti over. Bake 5 to 10 minutes or until surfaces are golden brown and cookies are dry. Remove biscotti to wire racks; cool completely.

Makes about 1½ dozen biscotti

Cherry Pistachio Biscotti

- 1 jar Cherry Pistachio Biscotti Mix
- 5 tablespoons butter, cut into pieces
- 1 egg
- 2 tablespoons milk or almond-flavored liqueur
- 1 teaspoon almond extract or vanilla

1. Preheat oven to 350°F. Lightly grease cookie sheet. Remove sugar packet from jar. Place remaining contents of jar in large bowl; stir until well blended. Cut in butter with pastry blender or two knives until mixture resembles coarse crumbs. Whisk together egg, milk and almond extract in small bowl. Add to flour mixture, stirring to form stiff dough. Knead dough in bowl. Divide dough in half; shape into two 9×2-inch logs. Place 2 inches apart on prepared cookie sheet. Sprinkle sugar over each log.

2. Bake 25 minutes or until logs are lightly browned. Cool logs on wire rack 15 minutes. *Reduce heat to 325°F.* Slice each log diagonally into ¾-inch-thick slices. Place slices, cut side up, on cookie sheet. Bake 10 minutes; turn biscotti over. Bake 5 to 10 minutes or until surfaces are golden brown and cookies are dry. Remove biscotti to wire racks; cool completely.

Makes about 1½ dozen biscotti

Cherry Pistachio Biscotti

- 1 jar Cherry Pistachio Biscotti Mix
- 5 tablespoons butter, cut into pieces
- 1 egg
- 2 tablespoons milk or almond-flavored liqueur
- 1 teaspoon almond extract or vanilla

1. Preheat oven to 350°F. Lightly grease cookie sheet. Remove sugar packet from jar. Place remaining contents of jar in large bowl; stir until well blended. Cut in butter with pastry blender or two knives until mixture resembles coarse crumbs. Whisk together egg, milk and almond extract in small bowl. Add to flour mixture, stirring to form stiff dough. Knead dough in bowl. Divide dough in half; shape into two 9×2-inch logs. Place 2 inches apart on prepared cookie sheet. Sprinkle sugar over each log.

2. Bake 25 minutes or until logs are lightly browned. Cool logs on wire rack 15 minutes. *Reduce heat to 325°F.* Slice each log diagonally into ¾-inch-thick slices. Place slices, cut side up, on cookie sheet. Bake 10 minutes; turn biscotti over. Bake 5 to 10 minutes or until surfaces are golden brown and cookies are dry. Remove biscotti to wire racks; cool completely.

Makes about 1½ dozen biscotti

Blissful Chocolate Biscotti Mix

- ¼ cup unsweetened cocoa powder
- 1¼ cups all-purpose flour
- ¾ teaspoon baking powder
- ½ teaspoon ground cinnamon
- ¼ teaspoon ground white pepper (optional)
- ¼ teaspoon salt
- ½ cup mini semisweet chocolate chips
- ½ cup whole blanched almonds, toasted* and cooled
- ½ cup packed brown sugar
- 1 tablespoon instant espresso powder *or* 2 tablespoons instant coffee granules
- ¼ cup granulated sugar

*To toast nuts, spread in single layer on baking sheet. Bake in preheated 350°F oven 8 to 10 minutes or until golden brown, stirring frequently.

1. Layer all ingredients in the order listed above in 1-quart food storage jar with tight-fitting lid.
2. Cover top of jar with fabric; attach gift tag with raffia or ribbon.

Makes 1 (1-quart) jar

Gift-Giving Tip

Share the holiday spirit with a unique gift bag filled with a beautifully decorated jar of Blissful Chocolate Biscotti Mix, a small bottle of almond-flavored liqueur, a variety of coffees or teas and special coffee mugs. Add a silicone baking mat for the baking enthusiast.

Blissful Chocolate Biscotti

1 jar Blissful Chocolate Biscotti Mix
2 eggs
¼ cup (½ stick) butter, softened
2 tablespoons almond-flavored liqueur or milk
1 teaspoon vanilla

1. Preheat oven to 350°F. Lightly grease cookie sheet. Place contents of jar in large bowl; stir until well blended. Beat eggs and butter in medium bowl with electric mixer on medium speed. Beat in liqueur and vanilla. Add to flour mixture, stirring to form stiff dough. Knead dough in bowl. Divide dough in half; shape into two 12×2-inch logs. Place logs 3 inches apart on prepared cookie sheet.

2. Bake 25 minutes or until logs are set. Cool logs on wire racks 15 minutes. *Reduce heat to 300°F.* Slice each log diagonally into ¾-inch-thick slices. Place biscotti, cut side up, on cookie sheet. Bake 15 minutes; turn biscotti over. Bake 10 to 15 minutes or until surfaces are dry. Remove biscotti to wire racks; cool completely.

Makes about 2 dozen biscotti

Blissful Chocolate Biscotti

- 1 jar Blissful Chocolate Biscotti Mix
- 2 eggs
- ¼ cup (½ stick) butter, softened
- 2 tablespoons almond-flavored liqueur or milk
- 1 teaspoon vanilla

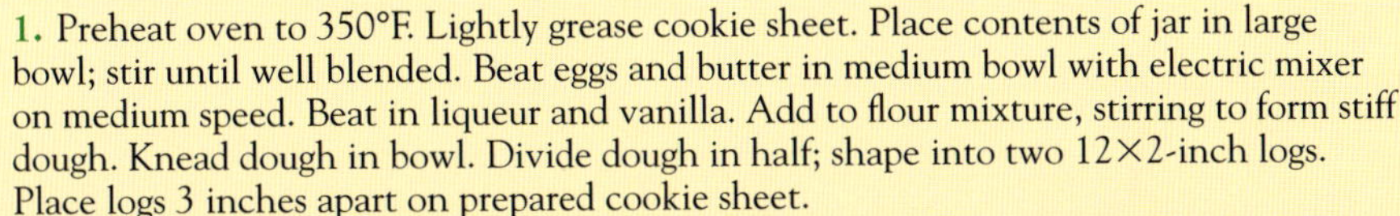

1. Preheat oven to 350°F. Lightly grease cookie sheet. Place contents of jar in large bowl; stir until well blended. Beat eggs and butter in medium bowl with electric mixer on medium speed. Beat in liqueur and vanilla. Add to flour mixture, stirring to form stiff dough. Knead dough in bowl. Divide dough in half; shape into two 12×2-inch logs. Place logs 3 inches apart on prepared cookie sheet.

2. Bake 25 minutes or until logs are set. Cool logs on wire racks 15 minutes. *Reduce heat to 300°F.* Slice each log diagonally into ¾-inch-thick slices. Place biscotti, cut side up, on cookie sheet. Bake 15 minutes; turn biscotti over. Bake 10 to 15 minutes or until surfaces are dry. Remove biscotti to wire racks; cool completely. *Makes about 2 dozen biscotti*

Blissful Chocolate Biscotti

- 1 jar Blissful Chocolate Biscotti Mix
- 2 eggs
- ¼ cup (½ stick) butter, softened
- 2 tablespoons almond-flavored liqueur or milk
- 1 teaspoon vanilla

1. Preheat oven to 350°F. Lightly grease cookie sheet. Place contents of jar in large bowl; stir until well blended. Beat eggs and butter in medium bowl with electric mixer on medium speed. Beat in liqueur and vanilla. Add to flour mixture, stirring to form stiff dough. Knead dough in bowl. Divide dough in half; shape into two 12×2-inch logs. Place logs 3 inches apart on prepared cookie sheet.

2. Bake 25 minutes or until logs are set. Cool logs on wire racks 15 minutes. *Reduce heat to 300°F.* Slice each log diagonally into ¾-inch-thick slices. Place biscotti, cut side up, on cookie sheet. Bake 15 minutes; turn biscotti over. Bake 10 to 15 minutes or until surfaces are dry. Remove biscotti to wire racks; cool completely. *Makes about 2 dozen biscotti*

Blissful Chocolate Biscotti

- 1 jar Blissful Chocolate Biscotti Mix
- 2 eggs
- ¼ cup (½ stick) butter, softened
- 2 tablespoons almond-flavored liqueur or milk
- 1 teaspoon vanilla

1. Preheat oven to 350°F. Lightly grease cookie sheet. Place contents of jar in large bowl; stir until well blended. Beat eggs and butter in medium bowl with electric mixer on medium speed. Beat in liqueur and vanilla. Add to flour mixture, stirring to form stiff dough. Knead dough in bowl. Divide dough in half; shape into two 12×2-inch logs. Place logs 3 inches apart on prepared cookie sheet.

2. Bake 25 minutes or until logs are set. Cool logs on wire racks 15 minutes. *Reduce heat to 300°F.* Slice each log diagonally into ¾-inch-thick slices. Place biscotti, cut side up, on cookie sheet. Bake 15 minutes; turn biscotti over. Bake 10 to 15 minutes or until surfaces are dry. Remove biscotti to wire racks; cool completely. *Makes about 2 dozen biscotti*

Blissful Chocolate Biscotti

1 jar Blissful Chocolate Biscotti Mix
2 eggs
¼ cup (½ stick) butter, softened
2 tablespoons almond-flavored liqueur or milk
1 teaspoon vanilla

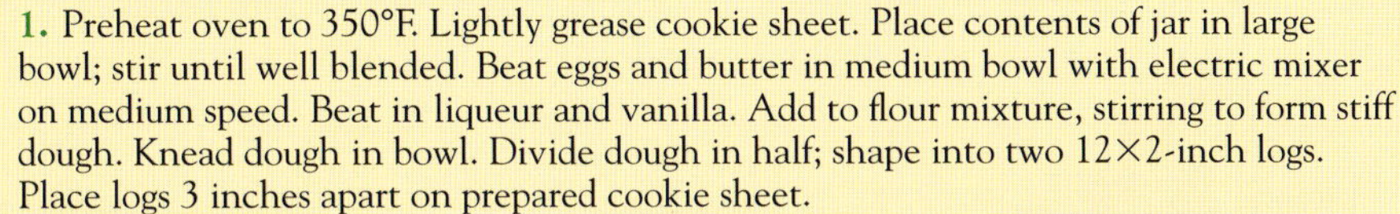

1. Preheat oven to 350°F. Lightly grease cookie sheet. Place contents of jar in large bowl; stir until well blended. Beat eggs and butter in medium bowl with electric mixer on medium speed. Beat in liqueur and vanilla. Add to flour mixture, stirring to form stiff dough. Knead dough in bowl. Divide dough in half; shape into two 12×2-inch logs. Place logs 3 inches apart on prepared cookie sheet.

2. Bake 25 minutes or until logs are set. Cool logs on wire racks 15 minutes. *Reduce heat to 300°F.* Slice each log diagonally into ¾-inch-thick slices. Place biscotti, cut side up, on cookie sheet. Bake 15 minutes; turn biscotti over. Bake 10 to 15 minutes or until surfaces are dry. Remove biscotti to wire racks; cool completely.

Makes about 2 dozen biscotti

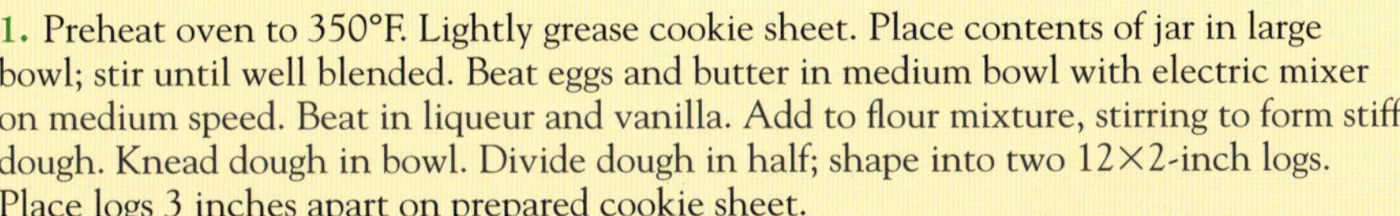

Blissful Chocolate Biscotti

1 jar Blissful Chocolate Biscotti Mix
2 eggs
¼ cup (½ stick) butter, softened
2 tablespoons almond-flavored liqueur or milk
1 teaspoon vanilla

1. Preheat oven to 350°F. Lightly grease cookie sheet. Place contents of jar in large bowl; stir until well blended. Beat eggs and butter in medium bowl with electric mixer on medium speed. Beat in liqueur and vanilla. Add to flour mixture, stirring to form stiff dough. Knead dough in bowl. Divide dough in half; shape into two 12×2-inch logs. Place logs 3 inches apart on prepared cookie sheet.

2. Bake 25 minutes or until logs are set. Cool logs on wire racks 15 minutes. *Reduce heat to 300°F.* Slice each log diagonally into ¾-inch-thick slices. Place biscotti, cut side up, on cookie sheet. Bake 15 minutes; turn biscotti over. Bake 10 to 15 minutes or until surfaces are dry. Remove biscotti to wire racks; cool completely.

Makes about 2 dozen biscotti

Blissful Chocolate Biscotti

1 jar Blissful Chocolate Biscotti Mix
2 eggs
¼ cup (½ stick) butter, softened
2 tablespoons almond-flavored liqueur or milk
1 teaspoon vanilla

1. Preheat oven to 350°F. Lightly grease cookie sheet. Place contents of jar in large bowl; stir until well blended. Beat eggs and butter in medium bowl with electric mixer on medium speed. Beat in liqueur and vanilla. Add to flour mixture, stirring to form stiff dough. Knead dough in bowl. Divide dough in half; shape into two 12×2-inch logs. Place logs 3 inches apart on prepared cookie sheet.

2. Bake 25 minutes or until logs are set. Cool logs on wire racks 15 minutes. *Reduce heat to 300°F.* Slice each log diagonally into ¾-inch-thick slices. Place biscotti, cut side up, on cookie sheet. Bake 15 minutes; turn biscotti over. Bake 10 to 15 minutes or until surfaces are dry. Remove biscotti to wire racks; cool completely.

Makes about 2 dozen biscotti

Snowy Date Nut Squares Mix

1¼ cups all-purpose flour
1 teaspoon dried orange peel
½ teaspoon baking powder
¼ teaspoon baking soda
¼ teaspoon salt
¼ teaspoon ground cinnamon
¼ teaspoon ground nutmeg
⅛ teaspoon ground cloves
1½ cups (8 ounces) finely chopped dates
¼ cup packed brown sugar
¼ cup granulated sugar
½ cup finely chopped toasted* walnuts
1 cup powdered sugar

*Place nuts in a microwavable dish. Microwave on HIGH 1 to 2 minutes or just until light golden brown, stirring nuts every 30 seconds. Allow to stand 3 minutes. Cool completely.

1. Layer all ingredients except powdered sugar in the order listed above in wide mouth 1-quart food storage jar with tight-fitting lid. Lightly pack down ingredients before adding another layer. Place powdered sugar in small plastic food storage bag. Close with twist tie; cut off top of bag. Place bag in jar.
2. Cover top of jar with fabric; attach gift tag with raffia or ribbon.

Makes 1 (1-quart) jar

Snowy Date Nut Squares

1 jar Snowy Date Nut Squares Mix
½ cup (1 stick) butter, softened
2 eggs
2 tablespoons orange juice

1. Preheat oven to 350°F. Spray 8-inch square baking pan with nonstick cooking spray.

2. Remove powdered sugar packet from jar. Pour remaining contents of jar into large bowl; stir until well blended. Beat butter in medium bowl with electric mixer on medium speed until smooth. Beat in eggs, one at a time. (Mixture may appear curdled.) Beat in orange juice. Add butter mixture to date-nut mixture; stir until well blended. Spread batter into prepared pan.

3. Bake 25 to 30 minutes or until toothpick inserted into center comes out clean. Cool slightly in pan on wire rack; cut into 1-inch squares. Place powdered sugar in small bowl. Roll warm cookies in powdered sugar, coating well. *Makes 36 (1-inch) squares*

Snowy Date Nut Squares

1 jar Snowy Date Nut Squares Mix
½ cup (1 stick) butter, softened
2 eggs
2 tablespoons orange juice

1. Preheat oven to 350°F. Spray 8-inch square baking pan with nonstick cooking spray.

2. Remove powdered sugar packet from jar. Pour remaining contents of jar into large bowl; stir until well blended. Beat butter in medium bowl with electric mixer on medium speed until smooth. Beat in eggs, one at a time. (Mixture may appear curdled.) Beat in orange juice. Add butter mixture to date-nut mixture; stir until well blended. Spread batter into prepared pan.

3. Bake 25 to 30 minutes or until toothpick inserted into center comes out clean. Cool slightly in pan on wire rack; cut into 1-inch squares. Place powdered sugar in small bowl. Roll warm cookies in powdered sugar, coating well. *Makes 36 (1-inch) squares*

Snowy Date Nut Squares

1 jar Snowy Date Nut Squares Mix
½ cup (1 stick) butter, softened
2 eggs
2 tablespoons orange juice

1. Preheat oven to 350°F. Spray 8-inch square baking pan with nonstick cooking spray.

2. Remove powdered sugar packet from jar. Pour remaining contents of jar into large bowl; stir until well blended. Beat butter in medium bowl with electric mixer on medium speed until smooth. Beat in eggs, one at a time. (Mixture may appear curdled.) Beat in orange juice. Add butter mixture to date-nut mixture; stir until well blended. Spread batter into prepared pan.

3. Bake 25 to 30 minutes or until toothpick inserted into center comes out clean. Cool slightly in pan on wire rack; cut into 1-inch squares. Place powdered sugar in small bowl. Roll warm cookies in powdered sugar, coating well. *Makes 36 (1-inch) squares*

Snowy Date Nut Squares

1 jar Snowy Date Nut Squares Mix
½ cup (1 stick) butter, softened
2 eggs
2 tablespoons orange juice

1. Preheat oven to 350°F. Spray 8-inch square baking pan with nonstick cooking spray.

2. Remove powdered sugar packet from jar. Pour remaining contents of jar into large bowl; stir until well blended. Beat butter in medium bowl with electric mixer on medium speed until smooth. Beat in eggs, one at a time. (Mixture may appear curdled.) Beat in orange juice. Add butter mixture to date-nut mixture; stir until well blended. Spread batter into prepared pan.

3. Bake 25 to 30 minutes or until toothpick inserted into center comes out clean. Cool slightly in pan on wire rack; cut into 1-inch squares. Place powdered sugar in small bowl. Roll warm cookies in powdered sugar, coating well. *Makes 36 (1-inch) squares*

Snowy Date Nut Squares

1 jar Snowy Date Nut Squares Mix
½ cup (1 stick) butter, softened
2 eggs
2 tablespoons orange juice

1. Preheat oven to 350°F. Spray 8-inch square baking pan with nonstick cooking spray.

2. Remove powdered sugar packet from jar. Pour remaining contents of jar into large bowl; stir until well blended. Beat butter in medium bowl with electric mixer on medium speed until smooth. Beat in eggs, one at a time. (Mixture may appear curdled.) Beat in orange juice. Add butter mixture to date-nut mixture; stir until well blended. Spread batter into prepared pan.

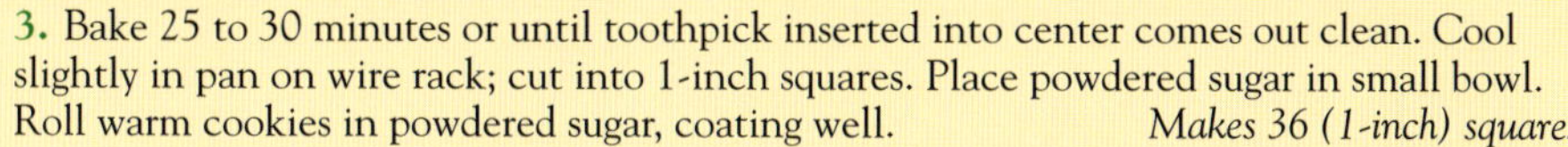

3. Bake 25 to 30 minutes or until toothpick inserted into center comes out clean. Cool slightly in pan on wire rack; cut into 1-inch squares. Place powdered sugar in small bowl. Roll warm cookies in powdered sugar, coating well. *Makes 36 (1-inch) squares*

Snowy Date Nut Squares

1 jar Snowy Date Nut Squares Mix
½ cup (1 stick) butter, softened
2 eggs
2 tablespoons orange juice

1. Preheat oven to 350°F. Spray 8-inch square baking pan with nonstick cooking spray.

2. Remove powdered sugar packet from jar. Pour remaining contents of jar into large bowl; stir until well blended. Beat butter in medium bowl with electric mixer on medium speed until smooth. Beat in eggs, one at a time. (Mixture may appear curdled.) Beat in orange juice. Add butter mixture to date-nut mixture; stir until well blended. Spread batter into prepared pan.

3. Bake 25 to 30 minutes or until toothpick inserted into center comes out clean. Cool slightly in pan on wire rack; cut into 1-inch squares. Place powdered sugar in small bowl. Roll warm cookies in powdered sugar, coating well. *Makes 36 (1-inch) squares*

Snowy Date Nut Squares

1 jar Snowy Date Nut Squares Mix
½ cup (1 stick) butter, softened
2 eggs
2 tablespoons orange juice

1. Preheat oven to 350°F. Spray 8-inch square baking pan with nonstick cooking spray.

2. Remove powdered sugar packet from jar. Pour remaining contents of jar into large bowl; stir until well blended. Beat butter in medium bowl with electric mixer on medium speed until smooth. Beat in eggs, one at a time. (Mixture may appear curdled.) Beat in orange juice. Add butter mixture to date-nut mixture; stir until well blended. Spread batter into prepared pan.

3. Bake 25 to 30 minutes or until toothpick inserted into center comes out clean. Cool slightly in pan on wire rack; cut into 1-inch squares. Place powdered sugar in small bowl. Roll warm cookies in powdered sugar, coating well. *Makes 36 (1-inch) squares*

Elfin Toffee Coffee Shortbread Mix

1¼ cups all-purpose flour
¼ teaspoon salt
½ cup toffee baking bits
¼ cup powdered sugar
⅓ cup semisweet chocolate chips
2 teaspoons instant espresso powder or instant coffee granules

1. Layer flour, salt, toffee bits and powdered sugar in 1-pint food storage jar with tight-fitting lid. Pack ingredients down before adding another layer. Place chocolate chips and espresso powder in separate small plastic food storage bags. Close each with twist tie; cut off tops of bags. Place bags in jar.
2. Cover top of jar with fabric; attach gift tag with raffia or ribbon.

Makes 1 (1-pint) jar

Gift-Giving Tip

Celebrate the holiday season with a festive gift basket. Include a beautifully decorated jar of Elfin Toffee Coffee Shortbread Mix, beverages of your choice and a special cookie plate for the baked shortbread.

Elfin Toffee Coffee Shortbread

- 1 jar Elfin Toffee Coffee Shortbread Mix
- 2 teaspoons vanilla
- ½ cup (1 stick) butter, softened

1. Preheat oven to 350°F. Lightly grease 8-inch square pan.
2. Remove chips and coffee packets from jar. Dissolve coffee granules in vanilla in small bowl. Place remaining contents of jar in large bowl; stir until well blended. Add butter and coffee mixture, stirring to form stiff dough. Press into prepared pan.
3. Bake 20 to 25 minutes or until lightly browned. Sprinkle chocolate chips over hot crust; let stand 1 minute to melt. Swirl melted chips over top. Cool in pan on wire rack.

Makes 2 to 3 dozen cookies

Serving Suggestion: For a fancy appearance, try cutting these delicious bars into diamond shapes. First, cut straight lines 1 inch apart the length of the baking pan, then cut straight lines 1½ inches apart diagonally across the pan.

Elfin Toffee Coffee Shortbread

1 jar Elfin Toffee Coffee Shortbread Mix
2 teaspoons vanilla
½ cup (1 stick) butter, softened

1. Preheat oven to 350°F. Lightly grease 8-inch square pan.

2. Remove chips and coffee packets from jar. Dissolve coffee granules in vanilla in small bowl. Place remaining contents of jar in large bowl; stir until well blended. Add butter and coffee mixture, stirring to form into stiff dough. Press into prepared pan.

3. Bake 20 to 25 minutes or until lightly browned. Sprinkle chocolate chips over hot crust; let stand 1 minute to melt. Swirl melted chips over top. Cool in pan on wire rack

Makes 2 to 3 dozen cookies

Serving Suggestion: For a fancy appearance, try cutting these delicious bars into diamond shapes. First, cut straight lines 1 inch apart the length of the baking pan, then cut straight lines 1½ inches apart diagonally across the pan.

Elfin Toffee Coffee Shortbread

1 jar Elfin Toffee Coffee Shortbread Mix
2 teaspoons vanilla
½ cup (1 stick) butter, softened

1. Preheat oven to 350°F. Lightly grease 8-inch square pan.

2. Remove chips and coffee packets from jar. Dissolve coffee granules in vanilla in small bowl. Place remaining contents of jar in large bowl; stir until well blended. Add butter and coffee mixture, stirring to form into stiff dough. Press into prepared pan.

3. Bake 20 to 25 minutes or until lightly browned. Sprinkle chocolate chips over hot crust; let stand 1 minute to melt. Swirl melted chips over top. Cool in pan on wire rack

Makes 2 to 3 dozen cookies

Serving Suggestion: For a fancy appearance, try cutting these delicious bars into diamond shapes. First, cut straight lines 1 inch apart the length of the baking pan, then cut straight lines 1½ inches apart diagonally across the pan.

Elfin Toffee Coffee Shortbread

1 jar Elfin Toffee Coffee Shortbread Mix
2 teaspoons vanilla
½ cup (1 stick) butter, softened

1. Preheat oven to 350°F. Lightly grease 8-inch square pan.

2. Remove chips and coffee packets from jar. Dissolve coffee granules in vanilla in small bowl. Place remaining contents of jar in large bowl; stir until well blended. Add butter and coffee mixture, stirring to form into stiff dough. Press into prepared pan.

3. Bake 20 to 25 minutes or until lightly browned. Sprinkle chocolate chips over hot crust; let stand 1 minute to melt. Swirl melted chips over top. Cool in pan on wire rack

Makes 2 to 3 dozen cookies

Serving Suggestion: For a fancy appearance, try cutting these delicious bars into diamond shapes. First, cut straight lines 1 inch apart the length of the baking pan, then cut straight lines 1½ inches apart diagonally across the pan.

Elfin Toffee Coffee Shortbread

1 jar Elfin Toffee Coffee Shortbread Mix
2 teaspoons vanilla
½ cup (1 stick) butter, softened

1. Preheat oven to 350°F. Lightly grease 8-inch square pan.
2. Remove chips and coffee packets from jar. Dissolve coffee granules in vanilla in small bowl. Place remaining contents of jar in large bowl; stir until well blended. Add butter and coffee mixture, stirring to form into stiff dough. Press into prepared pan.

3. Bake 20 to 25 minutes or until lightly browned. Sprinkle chocolate chips over hot crust; let stand 1 minute to melt. Swirl melted chips over top. Cool in pan on wire rack

Makes 2 to 3 dozen cookies

Serving Suggestion: For a fancy appearance, try cutting these delicious bars into diamond shapes. First, cut straight lines 1 inch apart the length of the baking pan, then cut straight lines 1½ inches apart diagonally across the pan.

Elfin Toffee Coffee Shortbread

1 jar Elfin Toffee Coffee Shortbread Mix
2 teaspoons vanilla
½ cup (1 stick) butter, softened

1. Preheat oven to 350°F. Lightly grease 8-inch square pan.
2. Remove chips and coffee packets from jar. Dissolve coffee granules in vanilla in small bowl. Place remaining contents of jar in large bowl; stir until well blended. Add butter and coffee mixture, stirring to form into stiff dough. Press into prepared pan.

3. Bake 20 to 25 minutes or until lightly browned. Sprinkle chocolate chips over hot crust; let stand 1 minute to melt. Swirl melted chips over top. Cool in pan on wire rack

Makes 2 to 3 dozen cookies

Serving Suggestion: For a fancy appearance, try cutting these delicious bars into diamond shapes. First, cut straight lines 1 inch apart the length of the baking pan, then cut straight lines 1½ inches apart diagonally across the pan.

Elfin Toffee Coffee Shortbread

1 jar Elfin Toffee Coffee Shortbread Mix
2 teaspoons vanilla
½ cup (1 stick) butter, softened

1. Preheat oven to 350°F. Lightly grease 8-inch square pan.
2. Remove chips and coffee packets from jar. Dissolve coffee granules in vanilla in small bowl. Place remaining contents of jar in large bowl; stir until well blended. Add butter and coffee mixture, stirring to form into stiff dough. Press into prepared pan.

3. Bake 20 to 25 minutes or until lightly browned. Sprinkle chocolate chips over hot crust; let stand 1 minute to melt. Swirl melted chips over top. Cool in pan on wire rack

Makes 2 to 3 dozen cookies

Serving Suggestion: For a fancy appearance, try cutting these delicious bars into diamond shapes. First, cut straight lines 1 inch apart the length of the baking pan, then cut straight lines 1½ inches apart diagonally across the pan.

Joyful Apricot Almond Bars Mix

1¾ cups all-purpose flour
2 teaspoons baking powder
1 cup chopped dried apricots or dried cherries
½ cup packed brown sugar
1 cup powdered sugar, divided
⅓ cup sliced almonds

1. Layer flour, baking powder, apricots, brown sugar and ½ cup powdered sugar in 1-quart food storage jar with tight-fitting lid. Place remaining ½ cup powdered sugar and almonds in separate small plastic food storage bags. Close with twist ties; cut off tops of bags. Place bags in jar.

2. Cover top of jar with fabric; attach gift tag with raffia or ribbon.

Makes 1 (1-quart) jar

Joyful Apricot Almond Bars

1 jar Joyful Apricot Almond Bars Mix
½ cup (1 stick) butter, softened
1 egg
1 teaspoon almond extract
1½ teaspoons milk

1. Preheat oven to 350°F. Grease 13×9-inch baking pan. Remove powdered sugar and almond packets from jar. Place remaining contents of jar in medium bowl; stir until well blended. Beat butter, egg and extract in large bowl with electric mixer on medium speed. (Mixture may appear curdled.) Add flour mixture; beat until just blended. (Dough will be crumbly.) Press dough into prepared pan; sprinkle with almonds. Bake 25 minutes until lightly browned. Cool in pan on wire rack.

2. Place powdered sugar in small bowl. Add enough milk to make glaze, stirring until smooth. Drizzle over warm cookies. Cool completely.

Makes about 3 to 4 dozen bars

Serving Suggestion: To cut these delicious bars into diamond shapes, cut straight lines 1 inch apart the length of the pan. Then, cut straight lines 1½ inches apart diagonally across the pan.

Joyful Apricot Almond Bars

1 jar Joyful Apricot Almond Bars Mix
½ cup (1 stick) butter, softened
1 egg
1 teaspoon almond extract
1½ teaspoons milk

1. Preheat oven to 350°F. Grease 13×9-inch baking pan. Remove powdered sugar and almond packets from jar. Place remaining contents of jar in medium bowl; stir until well blended. Beat butter, egg and extract in large bowl with electric mixer on medium speed. (Mixture may appear curdled.) Add flour mixture; beat until just blended. (Dough will be crumbly.) Press dough into prepared pan; sprinkle with almonds. Bake 25 minutes until lightly browned. Cool in pan on wire rack.

2. Place powdered sugar in small bowl. Add enough milk to make glaze, stirring until smooth. Drizzle over warm cookies. Cool completely. *Makes about 3 to 4 dozen bars*

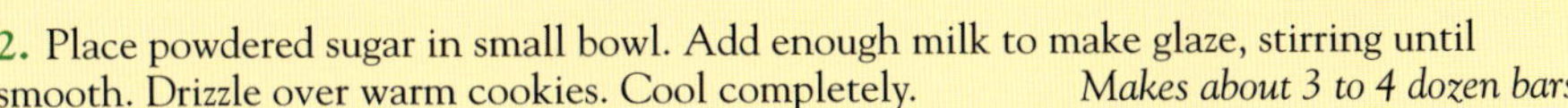

Serving Suggestion: To cut bars into diamond shapes, cut straight lines 1 inch apart the length of the pan. Then, cut straight lines 1½ inches apart diagonally across the pan.

Joyful Apricot Almond Bars

1 jar Joyful Apricot Almond Bars Mix
½ cup (1 stick) butter, softened
1 egg
1 teaspoon almond extract
1½ teaspoons milk

1. Preheat oven to 350°F. Grease 13×9-inch baking pan. Remove powdered sugar and almond packets from jar. Place remaining contents of jar in medium bowl; stir until well blended. Beat butter, egg and extract in large bowl with electric mixer on medium speed. (Mixture may appear curdled.) Add flour mixture; beat until just blended. (Dough will be crumbly.) Press dough into prepared pan; sprinkle with almonds. Bake 25 minutes until lightly browned. Cool in pan on wire rack.

2. Place powdered sugar in small bowl. Add enough milk to make glaze, stirring until smooth. Drizzle over warm cookies. Cool completely. *Makes about 3 to 4 dozen bars*

Serving Suggestion: To cut bars into diamond shapes, cut straight lines 1 inch apart the length of the pan. Then, cut straight lines 1½ inches apart diagonally across the pan.

Joyful Apricot Almond Bars

1 jar Joyful Apricot Almond Bars Mix
½ cup (1 stick) butter, softened
1 egg
1 teaspoon almond extract
1½ teaspoons milk

1. Preheat oven to 350°F. Grease 13×9-inch baking pan. Remove powdered sugar and almond packets from jar. Place remaining contents of jar in medium bowl; stir until well blended. Beat butter, egg and extract in large bowl with electric mixer on medium speed. (Mixture may appear curdled.) Add flour mixture; beat until just blended. (Dough will be crumbly.) Press dough into prepared pan; sprinkle with almonds. Bake 25 minutes until lightly browned. Cool in pan on wire rack.

2. Place powdered sugar in small bowl. Add enough milk to make glaze, stirring until smooth. Drizzle over warm cookies. Cool completely. *Makes about 3 to 4 dozen bars*

Serving Suggestion: To cut bars into diamond shapes, cut straight lines 1 inch apart the length of the pan. Then, cut straight lines 1½ inches apart diagonally across the pan.

Joyful Apricot Almond Bars

- 1 jar Joyful Apricot Almond Bars Mix
- ½ cup (1 stick) butter, softened
- 1 egg
- 1 teaspoon almond extract
- 1½ teaspoons milk

1. Preheat oven to 350°F. Grease 13×9-inch baking pan. Remove powdered sugar and almond packets from jar. Place remaining contents of jar in medium bowl; stir until well blended. Beat butter, egg and extract in large bowl with electric mixer on medium speed. (Mixture may appear curdled.) Add flour mixture; beat until just blended. (Dough will be crumbly.) Press dough into prepared pan; sprinkle with almonds. Bake 25 minutes until lightly browned. Cool in pan on wire rack.

2. Place powdered sugar in small bowl. Add enough milk to make glaze, stirring until smooth. Drizzle over warm cookies. Cool completely. *Makes about 3 to 4 dozen bars*

Serving Suggestion: To cut bars into diamond shapes, cut straight lines 1 inch apart the length of the pan. Then, cut straight lines 1½ inches apart diagonally across the pan.

Joyful Apricot Almond Bars

- 1 jar Joyful Apricot Almond Bars Mix
- ½ cup (1 stick) butter, softened
- 1 egg
- 1 teaspoon almond extract
- 1½ teaspoons milk

1. Preheat oven to 350°F. Grease 13×9-inch baking pan. Remove powdered sugar and almond packets from jar. Place remaining contents of jar in medium bowl; stir until well blended. Beat butter, egg and extract in large bowl with electric mixer on medium speed. (Mixture may appear curdled.) Add flour mixture; beat until just blended. (Dough will be crumbly.) Press dough into prepared pan; sprinkle with almonds. Bake 25 minutes until lightly browned. Cool in pan on wire rack.

2. Place powdered sugar in small bowl. Add enough milk to make glaze, stirring until smooth. Drizzle over warm cookies. Cool completely. *Makes about 3 to 4 dozen bars*

Serving Suggestion: To cut bars into diamond shapes, cut straight lines 1 inch apart the length of the pan. Then, cut straight lines 1½ inches apart diagonally across the pan.

Joyful Apricot Almond Bars

- 1 jar Joyful Apricot Almond Bars Mix
- ½ cup (1 stick) butter, softened
- 1 egg
- 1 teaspoon almond extract
- 1½ teaspoons milk

1. Preheat oven to 350°F. Grease 13×9-inch baking pan. Remove powdered sugar and almond packets from jar. Place remaining contents of jar in medium bowl; stir until well blended. Beat butter, egg and extract in large bowl with electric mixer on medium speed. (Mixture may appear curdled.) Add flour mixture; beat until just blended. (Dough will be crumbly.) Press dough into prepared pan; sprinkle with almonds. Bake 25 minutes until lightly browned. Cool in pan on wire rack.

2. Place powdered sugar in small bowl. Add enough milk to make glaze, stirring until smooth. Drizzle over warm cookies. Cool completely. *Makes about 3 to 4 dozen bars*

Serving Suggestion: To cut bars into diamond shapes, cut straight lines 1 inch apart the length of the pan. Then, cut straight lines 1½ inches apart diagonally across the pan.

Fudgy Chocolate-Amaretti Brownie Mix

- ⅔ cup unsweetened cocoa powder
- 1 cup all-purpose flour
- 1 teaspoon baking powder
- ¼ teaspoon salt
- ½ cup amaretti cookie crumbs
- ¾ cup granulated sugar
- ½ cup packed brown sugar
- ½ cup semisweet chocolate chips
- ⅓ cup powdered sugar

1. Layer all ingredients except powdered sugar in the order listed above in 1-quart food storage jar with tight-fitting lid. Lightly pack down ingredients before adding another layer. Place powdered sugar in small plastic food storage bag. Close with twist tie; cut off top of bag. Place bag in jar.
2. Cover top of jar with fabric; attach gift tag with raffia or ribbon.

Makes 1 (1-quart) jar

Fudgy Chocolate-Amaretti Brownies

- 1 jar Fudgy Chocolate-Amaretti Brownie Mix
- ½ cup (1 stick) butter, softened
- 1 teaspoon vanilla
- 2 eggs
- 2 tablespoons almond-flavored liqueur or milk
- Holiday-shaped stencil or doily with large pattern

1. Preheat oven to 350°F. Grease 9-inch square baking pan. Remove powdered sugar packet from jar. Place remaining contents of jar in large bowl; stir until well blended. Beat butter and vanilla in separate bowl with electric mixer on medium speed until smooth. Beat in eggs and liqueur. (Mixture may appear curdled.) Add to flour mixture; stir until well blended.

2. Spoon batter into prepared pan. (Batter will be thick and sticky. It will spread out during baking.) Bake 20 to 25 minutes or until brownies spring back when lightly touched. Do not overbake. Cool in pan on wire rack. Store, covered, in refrigerator for fudgy brownies. Before serving, place stencil on top of brownies. Dust with powdered sugar; remove stencil. Cut into bars.

Makes about 1½ dozen brownies

Fudgy Chocolate-Amaretti Brownies

- 1 jar Fudgy Chocolate-Amaretti Brownie Mix
- ½ cup (1 stick) butter, softened
- 1 teaspoon vanilla
- 2 eggs
- 2 tablespoons almond-flavored liqueur or milk
- Holiday-shaped stencil or doily with large pattern

1. Preheat oven to 350°F. Grease 9-inch square baking pan. Remove powdered sugar from jar. Place remaining contents of jar in large bowl; stir until well blended. Beat butter and vanilla in separate bowl with electric mixer on medium speed until smooth. Beat in eggs and liqueur. (Mixture may appear curdled.) Add to flour mixture; stir until well blended.

2. Spoon batter into prepared pan. (Batter will be thick and sticky. It will spread out during baking.) Bake 20 to 25 minutes or until brownies spring back when lightly touched. Do not overbake. Cool in pan on wire rack. Store, covered, in refrigerator for fudgy brownies. Before serving, place stencil on top of brownies. Dust with powdered sugar; remove stencil. Cut into bars.

Makes about 1½ dozen brownies

Fudgy Chocolate-Amaretti Brownies

- 1 jar Fudgy Chocolate-Amaretti Brownie Mix
- ½ cup (1 stick) butter, softened
- 1 teaspoon vanilla
- 2 eggs
- 2 tablespoons almond-flavored liqueur or milk
- Holiday-shaped stencil or doily with large pattern

1. Preheat oven to 350°F. Grease 9-inch square baking pan. Remove powdered sugar from jar. Place remaining contents of jar in large bowl; stir until well blended. Beat butter and vanilla in separate bowl with electric mixer on medium speed until smooth. Beat in eggs and liqueur. (Mixture may appear curdled.) Add to flour mixture; stir until well blended.

2. Spoon batter into prepared pan. (Batter will be thick and sticky. It will spread out during baking.) Bake 20 to 25 minutes or until brownies spring back when lightly touched. Do not overbake. Cool in pan on wire rack. Store, covered, in refrigerator for fudgy brownies. Before serving, place stencil on top of brownies. Dust with powdered sugar; remove stencil. Cut into bars.

Makes about 1½ dozen brownies

Fudgy Chocolate-Amaretti Brownies

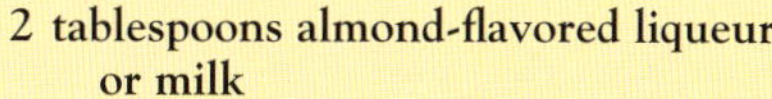

- 1 jar Fudgy Chocolate-Amaretti Brownie Mix
- ½ cup (1 stick) butter, softened
- 1 teaspoon vanilla
- 2 eggs
- 2 tablespoons almond-flavored liqueur or milk
- Holiday-shaped stencil or doily with large pattern

1. Preheat oven to 350°F. Grease 9-inch square baking pan. Remove powdered sugar from jar. Place remaining contents of jar in large bowl; stir until well blended. Beat butter and vanilla in separate bowl with electric mixer on medium speed until smooth. Beat in eggs and liqueur. (Mixture may appear curdled.) Add to flour mixture; stir until well blended.

2. Spoon batter into prepared pan. (Batter will be thick and sticky. It will spread out during baking.) Bake 20 to 25 minutes or until brownies spring back when lightly touched. Do not overbake. Cool in pan on wire rack. Store, covered, in refrigerator for fudgy brownies. Before serving, place stencil on top of brownies. Dust with powdered sugar; remove stencil. Cut into bars.

Makes about 1½ dozen brownies

Fudgy Chocolate-Amaretti Brownies

- 1 jar Fudgy Chocolate-Amaretti Brownie Mix
- ½ cup (1 stick) butter, softened
- 1 teaspoon vanilla
- 2 eggs
- 2 tablespoons almond-flavored liqueur or milk
- Holiday-shaped stencil or doily with large pattern

1. Preheat oven to 350°F. Grease 9-inch square baking pan. Remove powdered sugar from jar. Place remaining contents of jar in large bowl; stir until well blended. Beat butter and vanilla in separate bowl with electric mixer on medium speed until smooth. Beat in eggs and liqueur. (Mixture may appear curdled.) Add to flour mixture; stir until well blended.

2. Spoon batter into prepared pan. (Batter will be thick and sticky. It will spread out during baking.) Bake 20 to 25 minutes or until brownies spring back when lightly touched. Do not overbake. Cool in pan on wire rack. Store, covered, in refrigerator for fudgy brownies. Before serving, place stencil on top of brownies. Dust with powdered sugar; remove stencil. Cut into bars.

Makes about 1½ dozen brownies

Fudgy Chocolate-Amaretti Brownies

- 1 jar Fudgy Chocolate-Amaretti Brownie Mix
- ½ cup (1 stick) butter, softened
- 1 teaspoon vanilla
- 2 eggs
- 2 tablespoons almond-flavored liqueur or milk
- Holiday-shaped stencil or doily with large pattern

1. Preheat oven to 350°F. Grease 9-inch square baking pan. Remove powdered sugar from jar. Place remaining contents of jar in large bowl; stir until well blended. Beat butter and vanilla in separate bowl with electric mixer on medium speed until smooth. Beat in eggs and liqueur. (Mixture may appear curdled.) Add to flour mixture; stir until well blended.

2. Spoon batter into prepared pan. (Batter will be thick and sticky. It will spread out during baking.) Bake 20 to 25 minutes or until brownies spring back when lightly touched. Do not overbake. Cool in pan on wire rack. Store, covered, in refrigerator for fudgy brownies. Before serving, place stencil on top of brownies. Dust with powdered sugar; remove stencil. Cut into bars.

Makes about 1½ dozen brownies

Fudgy Chocolate-Amaretti Brownies

- 1 jar Fudgy Chocolate-Amaretti Brownie Mix
- ½ cup (1 stick) butter, softened
- 1 teaspoon vanilla
- 2 eggs
- 2 tablespoons almond-flavored liqueur or milk
- Holiday-shaped stencil or doily with large pattern

1. Preheat oven to 350°F. Grease 9-inch square baking pan. Remove powdered sugar from jar. Place remaining contents of jar in large bowl; stir until well blended. Beat butter and vanilla in separate bowl with electric mixer on medium speed until smooth. Beat in eggs and liqueur. (Mixture may appear curdled.) Add to flour mixture; stir until well blended.

2. Spoon batter into prepared pan. (Batter will be thick and sticky. It will spread out during baking.) Bake 20 to 25 minutes or until brownies spring back when lightly touched. Do not overbake. Cool in pan on wire rack. Store, covered, in refrigerator for fudgy brownies. Before serving, place stencil on top of brownies. Dust with powdered sugar; remove stencil. Cut into bars.

Makes about 1½ dozen brownies

Toasty Rosemary Nut Mix

1 cup whole pecans
1½ teaspoons rosemary, crushed
¾ teaspoon garlic salt
½ teaspoon paprika
¼ teaspoon ground red pepper
1 cup whole walnuts

1. Layer all ingredients in the order listed above in 1-pint food storage jar with tight-fitting lid. Shake jar to mix seasonings.
2. Cover top of jar with fabric; attach gift tag with raffia or ribbon.

Makes 1 (1-pint) jar

Gift-Giving Tip

Embellish the traditional bottle of wine hostess gift with a gift jar of Toasty Rosemary Nuts and a pretty cut-glass container—a lasting remembrance of your thoughtful gift.

Toasty Rosemary Nuts

1 jar Toasty Rosemary Nut Mix
2 tablespoons butter

Place butter in microwavable baking dish; add contents of jar. Microwave on HIGH 2 minutes, stirring every 30 seconds until nuts are golden brown. Spread nuts on paper towels to cool.

Makes 2 cups nuts

Toasty Cranberry Rosemary Nuts: Stir ½ cup dried cranberries into cooled nuts.

Serving Suggestion: Serve nuts in leafy green salad with apples and blue cheese.

Toasty Rosemary Nuts

1 jar Toasty Rosemary Nut Mix **2 tablespoons butter**

Place butter in microwavable baking dish; add contents of jar. Microwave on HIGH 2 minutes, stirring every 30 seconds until nuts are golden brown. Spread nuts on paper towels to cool.

Makes 2 cups nuts

Toasty Cranberry Rosemary Nuts: Stir ½ cup dried cranberries into cooled nuts.

Serving Suggestion: Serve nuts in leafy green salad with apples and blue cheese.

Toasty Rosemary Nuts

1 jar Toasty Rosemary Nut Mix **2 tablespoons butter**

Place butter in microwavable baking dish; add contents of jar. Microwave on HIGH 2 minutes, stirring every 30 seconds until nuts are golden brown. Spread nuts on paper towels to cool.

Makes 2 cups nuts

Toasty Cranberry Rosemary Nuts: Stir ½ cup dried cranberries into cooled nuts.

Serving Suggestion: Serve nuts in leafy green salad with apples and blue cheese.

Toasty Rosemary Nuts

1 jar Toasty Rosemary Nut Mix **2 tablespoons butter**

Place butter in microwavable baking dish; add contents of jar. Microwave on HIGH 2 minutes, stirring every 30 seconds until nuts are golden brown. Spread nuts on paper towels to cool.

Makes 2 cups nuts

Toasty Cranberry Rosemary Nuts: Stir ½ cup dried cranberries into cooled nuts.

Serving Suggestion: Serve nuts in leafy green salad with apples and blue cheese.

Toasty Rosemary Nuts

1 jar Toasty Rosemary Nut Mix **2 tablespoons butter**

Place butter in microwavable baking dish; add contents of jar. Microwave on HIGH 2 minutes, stirring every 30 seconds until nuts are golden brown. Spread nuts on paper towels to cool.

Makes 2 cups nuts

Toasty Cranberry Rosemary Nuts: Stir ½ cup dried cranberries into cooled nuts.

Serving Suggestion: Serve nuts in leafy green salad with apples and blue cheese.

Toasty Rosemary Nuts

1 jar Toasty Rosemary Nut Mix **2 tablespoons butter**

Place butter in microwavable baking dish; add contents of jar. Microwave on HIGH 2 minutes, stirring every 30 seconds until nuts are golden brown. Spread nuts on paper towels to cool.

Makes 2 cups nuts

Toasty Cranberry Rosemary Nuts: Stir ½ cup dried cranberries into cooled nuts.

Serving Suggestion: Serve nuts in leafy green salad with apples and blue cheese.

Toasty Rosemary Nuts

1 jar Toasty Rosemary Nut Mix **2 tablespoons butter**

Place butter in microwavable baking dish; add contents of jar. Microwave on HIGH 2 minutes, stirring every 30 seconds until nuts are golden brown. Spread nuts on paper towels to cool.

Makes 2 cups nuts

Toasty Cranberry Rosemary Nuts: Stir ½ cup dried cranberries into cooled nuts.

Serving Suggestion: Serve nuts in leafy green salad with apples and blue cheese.

Jolly Party Mix

- 2 cups bite-size corn or rice cereal
- 2 cups (½ package) bagel chips, broken in half
- 1½ cups pretzel twists
- 1 cup oyster crackers
- 1 cup pistachio nuts
- ¼ cup grated Parmesan cheese
- 1 package (1 ounce) dry ranch salad dressing mix
- ½ teaspoon garlic powder
- ⅛ teaspoon ground red pepper

1. Layer cereal, chips, pretzels, crackers, nuts and cheese attractively in any order in 2-quart food storage jar with tight-fitting lid. Place dressing mix, garlic powder and red pepper in small plastic food storage bag. Close with twist tie; cut off top of bag. Place bag in jar.
2. Cover top of jar with fabric; attach gift tag with raffia or ribbon.

Makes 1 (2-quart) jar

Jolly Party Mix

1 jar Jolly Party Mix
¼ cup (½ stick) butter

1. Preheat oven to 300°F. Remove seasoning mix from jar. Place contents of jar in large bowl. Melt butter in small saucepan. Add seasoning mix; stir until blended. Drizzle over cereal mixture; toss to coat.

2. Spread mixture in single layer on jelly-roll pan. Bake 20 to 30 minutes or until mixture is lightly browned, stirring every 15 minutes. Cool completely in pan on wire rack. Store in airtight container at room temperature up to 2 weeks.

Makes about 6 cups party mix

Variation: Stir 1 cup dried cranberries into cooled mix for a colorful variation.

Jolly Party Mix

1 jar Jolly Party Mix

¼ cup (½ stick) butter

1. Preheat oven to 300°F. Remove seasoning mix from jar. Place contents of jar in large bowl. Melt butter in small saucepan. Add seasoning mix; stir until blended. Drizzle over cereal mixture; toss to coat.

2. Spread mixture in single layer on jelly-roll pan. Bake 20 to 30 minutes or until mixture is lightly browned, stirring every 15 minutes. Cool completely in pan on wire rack. Store in airtight container at room temperature up to 2 weeks.

Makes about 6 cups party mix

Variation: Stir 1 cup dried cranberries into cooled mix for a colorful variation.

Jolly Party Mix

1 jar Jolly Party Mix

¼ cup (½ stick) butter

1. Preheat oven to 300°F. Remove seasoning mix from jar. Place contents of jar in large bowl. Melt butter in small saucepan. Add seasoning mix; stir until blended. Drizzle over cereal mixture; toss to coat.

2. Spread mixture in single layer on jelly-roll pan. Bake 20 to 30 minutes or until mixture is lightly browned, stirring every 15 minutes. Cool completely in pan on wire rack. Store in airtight container at room temperature up to 2 weeks.

Makes about 6 cups party mix

Variation: Stir 1 cup dried cranberries into cooled mix for a colorful variation.

Jolly Party Mix

1 jar Jolly Party Mix
¼ cup (½ stick) butter

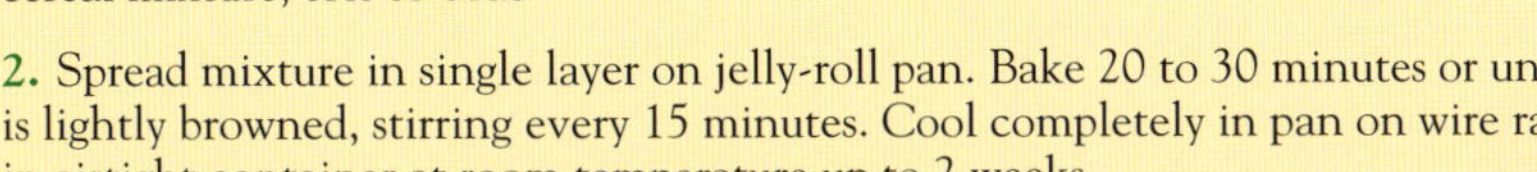

1. Preheat oven to 300°F. Remove seasoning mix from jar. Place contents of jar in large bowl. Melt butter in small saucepan. Add seasoning mix; stir until blended. Drizzle over cereal mixture; toss to coat.

2. Spread mixture in single layer on jelly-roll pan. Bake 20 to 30 minutes or until mixture is lightly browned, stirring every 15 minutes. Cool completely in pan on wire rack. Store in airtight container at room temperature up to 2 weeks.

Makes about 6 cups party mix

Variation: Stir 1 cup dried cranberries into cooled mix for a colorful variation.

Jolly Party Mix

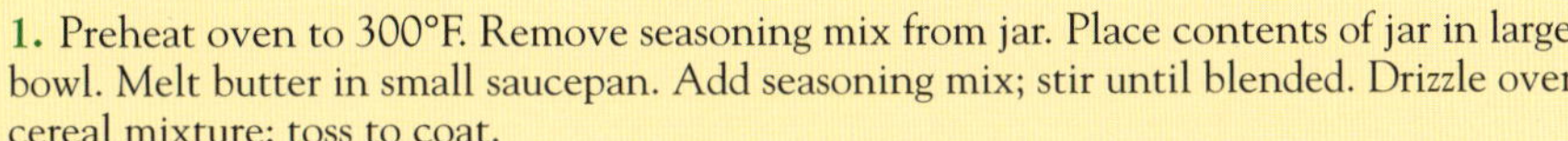

1 jar Jolly Party Mix
¼ cup (½ stick) butter

1. Preheat oven to 300°F. Remove seasoning mix from jar. Place contents of jar in large bowl. Melt butter in small saucepan. Add seasoning mix; stir until blended. Drizzle over cereal mixture; toss to coat.

2. Spread mixture in single layer on jelly-roll pan. Bake 20 to 30 minutes or until mixture is lightly browned, stirring every 15 minutes. Cool completely in pan on wire rack. Store in airtight container at room temperature up to 2 weeks.

Makes about 6 cups party mix

Variation: Stir 1 cup dried cranberries into cooled mix for a colorful variation.

Jolly Party Mix

1 jar Jolly Party Mix
¼ cup (½ stick) butter

1. Preheat oven to 300°F. Remove seasoning mix from jar. Place contents of jar in large bowl. Melt butter in small saucepan. Add seasoning mix; stir until blended. Drizzle over cereal mixture; toss to coat.

2. Spread mixture in single layer on jelly-roll pan. Bake 20 to 30 minutes or until mixture is lightly browned, stirring every 15 minutes. Cool completely in pan on wire rack. Store in airtight container at room temperature up to 2 weeks.

Makes about 6 cups party mix

Variation: Stir 1 cup dried cranberries into cooled mix for a colorful variation.

Glorious Sugared Nut Mix

½ cup whole blanched almonds, toasted* and cooled
1 bar (7 ounces) milk chocolate, broken into pieces
1 cup whole pecans, toasted* and cooled
2 tablespoons unsweetened cocoa powder
2 teaspoons ground cinnamon
½ cup powdered sugar

*Place nuts in a microwavable dish. Microwave on HIGH 1 to 2 minutes or just until light golden brown, stirring nuts every 30 seconds. Allow to stand 3 minutes. Cool completely.

1. Layer almonds, chocolate pieces and pecans in 1-pint food storage jar with tight-fitting lid. Place cocoa and cinnamon in small plastic food storage bag. Place powdered sugar in second bag. Close each bag with twist tie; cut off tops of bags. Place bags in jar.
2. Cover top of jar with fabric; attach gift tag with raffia or ribbon.

Makes 1 (1-pint) jar

Coffee-Flavored Sugared Nuts: Add 1 tablespoon instant espresso powder or instant coffee granules to bag of cocoa and cinnamon.

Gift-Giving Tip

For an extra touch of holiday magic, give a jar of Glorious Sugared Nut Mix along with a sparkling glass or vintage candy dish—the perfect gift for both old and new friends.

Glorious Sugared Nuts

1 jar Glorious Sugared Nut Mix

1. Line baking sheet with foil. Set aside.

2. Remove powdered sugar and cocoa packets from jar. Place remaining contents of jar into medium nonstick skillet. Stir mixture over medium heat until chocolate is melted and nuts are coated with chocolate. Remove skillet from heat. Sprinkle cocoa mixture over nuts; stir to coat.

3. Place powdered sugar in medium bowl. Add nuts; stir to coat with sugar. Separate into small pieces. Spread on prepared baking sheet to cool. Store in tightly covered container.

Makes about 1½ cups nuts

Glorious Sugared Nuts

1 jar Glorious Sugared Nut Mix

1. Line baking sheet with foil. Set aside.

2. Remove powdered sugar and cocoa packets from jar. Place remaining contents of jar into medium nonstick skillet. Stir mixture over medium heat until chocolate is melted and nuts are coated with chocolate. Remove skillet from heat. Sprinkle cocoa mixture over nuts; stir to coat.

3. Place powdered sugar in medium bowl. Add nuts; stir to coat with sugar. Separate into small pieces. Spread on prepared baking sheet to cool. Store in tightly covered container.

Makes about 1½ cups nuts

Glorious Sugared Nuts

1 jar Glorious Sugared Nut Mix

1. Line baking sheet with foil. Set aside.

2. Remove powdered sugar and cocoa packets from jar. Place remaining contents of jar into medium nonstick skillet. Stir mixture over medium heat until chocolate is melted and nuts are coated with chocolate. Remove skillet from heat. Sprinkle cocoa mixture over nuts; stir to coat.

3. Place powdered sugar in medium bowl. Add nuts; stir to coat with sugar. Separate into small pieces. Spread on prepared baking sheet to cool. Store in tightly covered container.

Makes about 1½ cups nuts

Glorious Sugared Nuts

1 jar Glorious Sugared Nut Mix

1. Line baking sheet with foil. Set aside.

2. Remove powdered sugar and cocoa packets from jar. Place remaining contents of jar into medium nonstick skillet. Stir mixture over medium heat until chocolate is melted and nuts are coated with chocolate. Remove skillet from heat. Sprinkle cocoa mixture over nuts; stir to coat.

3. Place powdered sugar in medium bowl. Add nuts; stir to coat with sugar. Separate into small pieces. Spread on prepared baking sheet to cool. Store in tightly covered container.

Makes about 1½ cups nuts

Glorious Sugared Nuts

1 jar Glorious Sugared Nut Mix

1. Line baking sheet with foil. Set aside.

2. Remove powdered sugar and cocoa packets from jar. Place remaining contents of jar into medium nonstick skillet. Stir mixture over medium heat until chocolate is melted and nuts are coated with chocolate. Remove skillet from heat. Sprinkle cocoa mixture over nuts; stir to coat.

3. Place powdered sugar in medium bowl. Add nuts; stir to coat with sugar. Separate into small pieces. Spread on prepared baking sheet to cool. Store in tightly covered container.

Makes about 1½ cups nuts

Glorious Sugared Nuts

1 jar Glorious Sugared Nut Mix

1. Line baking sheet with foil. Set aside.

2. Remove powdered sugar and cocoa packets from jar. Place remaining contents of jar into medium nonstick skillet. Stir mixture over medium heat until chocolate is melted and nuts are coated with chocolate. Remove skillet from heat. Sprinkle cocoa mixture over nuts; stir to coat.

3. Place powdered sugar in medium bowl. Add nuts; stir to coat with sugar. Separate into small pieces. Spread on prepared baking sheet to cool. Store in tightly covered container.

Makes about 1½ cups nuts

Glorious Sugared Nuts

1 jar Glorious Sugared Nut Mix

1. Line baking sheet with foil. Set aside.

2. Remove powdered sugar and cocoa packets from jar. Place remaining contents of jar into medium nonstick skillet. Stir mixture over medium heat until chocolate is melted and nuts are coated with chocolate. Remove skillet from heat. Sprinkle cocoa mixture over nuts; stir to coat.

3. Place powdered sugar in medium bowl. Add nuts; stir to coat with sugar. Separate into small pieces. Spread on prepared baking sheet to cool. Store in tightly covered container.

Makes about 1½ cups nuts

Yuletide Cheddar Crisps Mix

1 cup all-purpose flour
¾ teaspoon granulated sugar
¾ teaspoon salt
½ teaspoon baking soda
½ cup yellow cornmeal
½ cup all-purpose flour

1. Layer all ingredients in the order listed above in 1-pint food storage jar with tight-fitting lid.
2. Cover top of jar with fabric; attach gift tag with raffia or ribbon.

Makes 1 (1-pint) jar

Yuletide Cheddar Crisps

1 jar Yuletide Cheddar Crisps Mix
½ cup (1 stick) butter, cut into bits
1½ cups (6 ounces) shredded sharp Cheddar cheese
½ cup cold water
2 tablespoons white vinegar
Coarsely ground black pepper

1. Preheat oven to 375°F. Grease 2 large baking sheets. Place contents of jar in large bowl. Cut in butter with pastry blender until mixture resembles coarse crumbs. Stir in cheese, water and vinegar with fork until mixture forms soft dough. Cover dough; refrigerate 1 hour or freeze 30 minutes until firm.

2. Divide dough into 4 equal portions. Roll each piece into paper-thin circle (about 13 inches in diameter) on floured surface. (Dough must be very thin.) Sprinkle with pepper; press pepper firmly into dough. Cut each circle into 8 wedges; place wedges on prepared baking sheets. Bake about 10 minutes or until crisp. Store in airtight container for up to 3 days. *Makes 32 crisps*

Yuletide Cheddar Crisps

1 jar Yuletide Cheddar Crisps Mix
½ cup (1 stick) butter, cut into bits
1½ cups (6 ounces) shredded sharp Cheddar cheese
½ cup cold water
2 tablespoons white vinegar
Coarsely ground black pepper

1. Preheat oven to 375°F. Grease 2 large baking sheets. Place contents of jar in large bowl. Cut in butter with pastry blender until mixture resembles coarse crumbs. Stir in cheese, water and vinegar with fork until mixture forms soft dough. Cover dough; refrigerate 1 hour or freeze 30 minutes until firm.

2. Divide dough into 4 equal portions. Roll each piece into paper-thin circle (about 13 inches in diameter) on floured surface. (Dough must be very thin.) Sprinkle with pepper; press pepper firmly into dough. Cut each circle into 8 wedges; place wedges on prepared baking sheets. Bake about 10 minutes or until crisp. Store in airtight container for up to 3 days.

Makes 32 crisps

Yuletide Cheddar Crisps

1 jar Yuletide Cheddar Crisps Mix
½ cup (1 stick) butter, cut into bits
1½ cups (6 ounces) shredded sharp Cheddar cheese
½ cup cold water
2 tablespoons white vinegar
Coarsely ground black pepper

1. Preheat oven to 375°F. Grease 2 large baking sheets. Place contents of jar in large bowl. Cut in butter with pastry blender until mixture resembles coarse crumbs. Stir in cheese, water and vinegar with fork until mixture forms soft dough. Cover dough; refrigerate 1 hour or freeze 30 minutes until firm.

2. Divide dough into 4 equal portions. Roll each piece into paper-thin circle (about 13 inches in diameter) on floured surface. (Dough must be very thin.) Sprinkle with pepper; press pepper firmly into dough. Cut each circle into 8 wedges; place wedges on prepared baking sheets. Bake about 10 minutes or until crisp. Store in airtight container for up to 3 days.

Makes 32 crisps

Yuletide Cheddar Crisps

1 jar Yuletide Cheddar Crisps Mix
½ cup (1 stick) butter, cut into bits
1½ cups (6 ounces) shredded sharp Cheddar cheese
½ cup cold water
2 tablespoons white vinegar
Coarsely ground black pepper

1. Preheat oven to 375°F. Grease 2 large baking sheets. Place contents of jar in large bowl. Cut in butter with pastry blender until mixture resembles coarse crumbs. Stir in cheese, water and vinegar with fork until mixture forms soft dough. Cover dough; refrigerate 1 hour or freeze 30 minutes until firm.

2. Divide dough into 4 equal portions. Roll each piece into paper-thin circle (about 13 inches in diameter) on floured surface. (Dough must be very thin.) Sprinkle with pepper; press pepper firmly into dough. Cut each circle into 8 wedges; place wedges on prepared baking sheets. Bake about 10 minutes or until crisp. Store in airtight container for up to 3 days.

Makes 32 crisps

Yuletide Cheddar Crisps

1 jar Yuletide Cheddar Crisps Mix
½ cup (1 stick) butter, cut into bits
1½ cups (6 ounces) shredded sharp Cheddar cheese
½ cup cold water
2 tablespoons white vinegar
Coarsely ground black pepper

1. Preheat oven to 375°F. Grease 2 large baking sheets. Place contents of jar in large bowl. Cut in butter with pastry blender until mixture resembles coarse crumbs. Stir in cheese, water and vinegar with fork until mixture forms soft dough. Cover dough; refrigerate 1 hour or freeze 30 minutes until firm.

2. Divide dough into 4 equal portions. Roll each piece into paper-thin circle (about 13 inches in diameter) on floured surface. (Dough must be very thin.) Sprinkle with pepper; press pepper firmly into dough. Cut each circle into 8 wedges; place wedges on prepared baking sheets. Bake about 10 minutes or until crisp. Store in airtight container for up to 3 days.

Makes 32 crisps

Yuletide Cheddar Crisps

1 jar Yuletide Cheddar Crisps Mix
½ cup (1 stick) butter, cut into bits
1½ cups (6 ounces) shredded sharp Cheddar cheese
½ cup cold water
2 tablespoons white vinegar
Coarsely ground black pepper

1. Preheat oven to 375°F. Grease 2 large baking sheets. Place contents of jar in large bowl. Cut in butter with pastry blender until mixture resembles coarse crumbs. Stir in cheese, water and vinegar with fork until mixture forms soft dough. Cover dough; refrigerate 1 hour or freeze 30 minutes until firm.

2. Divide dough into 4 equal portions. Roll each piece into paper-thin circle (about 13 inches in diameter) on floured surface. (Dough must be very thin.) Sprinkle with pepper; press pepper firmly into dough. Cut each circle into 8 wedges; place wedges on prepared baking sheets. Bake about 10 minutes or until crisp. Store in airtight container for up to 3 days.

Makes 32 crisps

Yuletide Cheddar Crisps

1 jar Yuletide Cheddar Crisps Mix
½ cup (1 stick) butter, cut into bits
1½ cups (6 ounces) shredded sharp Cheddar cheese
½ cup cold water
2 tablespoons white vinegar
Coarsely ground black pepper

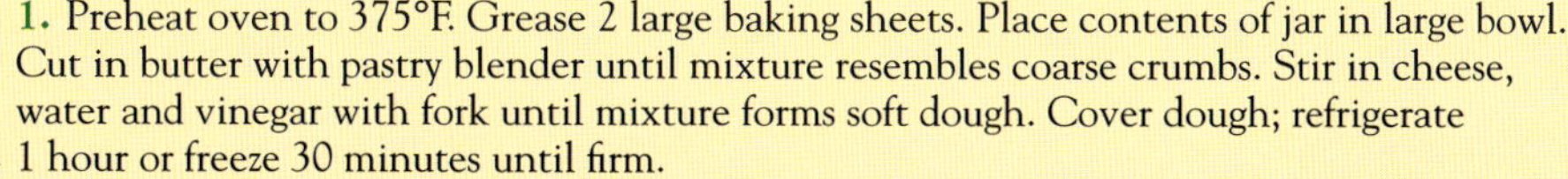

1. Preheat oven to 375°F. Grease 2 large baking sheets. Place contents of jar in large bowl. Cut in butter with pastry blender until mixture resembles coarse crumbs. Stir in cheese, water and vinegar with fork until mixture forms soft dough. Cover dough; refrigerate 1 hour or freeze 30 minutes until firm.

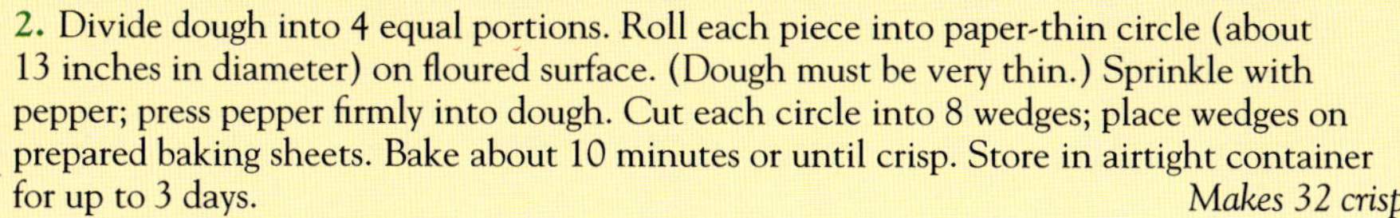

2. Divide dough into 4 equal portions. Roll each piece into paper-thin circle (about 13 inches in diameter) on floured surface. (Dough must be very thin.) Sprinkle with pepper; press pepper firmly into dough. Cut each circle into 8 wedges; place wedges on prepared baking sheets. Bake about 10 minutes or until crisp. Store in airtight container for up to 3 days.

Makes 32 crisps

Santa's Peppermint Chocolates Mix

1 cup (6 ounces) semisweet chocolate chips
¼ cup white chocolate chips
½ cup milk chocolate chips
¼ cup crushed peppermint candy (about 10 peppermint candy rounds)

1. Layer all ingredients except peppermint in the order listed above in 1-pint food storage jar with tight-fitting lid. Place peppermint in small plastic food storage bag. Close with twist tie; cut off top of bag. Place bag in jar.
2. Cover top of jar with fabric; attach gift tag with raffia or ribbon.

Makes 1 (1-pint) jar

Tip: To crush candies, place candies in plastic food storage bag. Crush with rolling pin or mallet. Or, process in food processor using pulsing action.

Gift-Giving Tip

Share the holiday spirit with beautifully decorated gifts. Look for inexpensive antique plates, relish trays or vintage glassware at flea markets or antique stores. Assemble with a decorated gift jar in a holiday package. Tie with a generous bow for a simple yet spectacular gift.

Santa's Peppermint Chocolates

1 jar Santa's Peppermint Chocolates Mix

1. Line 8-inch square baking pan with buttered foil. Set aside.
2. Remove peppermint. Place remaining contents of jar in microwavable 2-cup glass measuring cup. Microwave on HIGH 1 to 2 minutes, stirring after every 30 seconds until chips are melted. Spoon chocolate into prepared pan spreading evenly over bottom to within ½ inch of sides. Sprinkle with peppermint; press into chocolate.
3. Refrigerate until almost firm before cutting into squares. Refrigerate until firm before removing foil. *Makes about 3 dozen*

Serving Suggestions: Peppermints are easier to cut into squares if chocolate is not completely firm. For a festive presentation, place individual candy pieces in paper or foil candy cups.

Santa's Peppermint Chocolates

1 jar Santa's Peppermint Chocolates Mix

1. Line 8-inch square baking pan with buttered foil. Set aside.

2. Remove peppermint. Place remaining contents of jar in microwavable 2-cup glass measuring cup. Microwave on HIGH 1 to 2 minutes, stirring after every 30 seconds until chips are melted. Spoon chocolate into prepared pan spreading evenly over bottom to within ½ inch of sides. Sprinkle with peppermint; press into chocolate.

3. Refrigerate until almost firm before cutting into squares. Refrigerate until firm before removing foil.

Makes about 3 dozen

Serving Suggestions: Peppermints are easier to cut into squares if chocolate is not completely firm. For a festive presentation, place individual candy pieces in paper or foil candy cups.

Santa's Peppermint Chocolates

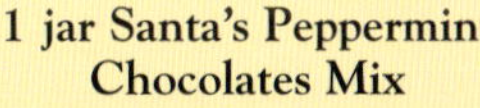

1 jar Santa's Peppermint Chocolates Mix

1. Line 8-inch square baking pan with buttered foil. Set aside.

2. Remove peppermint. Place remaining contents of jar in microwavable 2-cup glass measuring cup. Microwave on HIGH 1 to 2 minutes, stirring after every 30 seconds until chips are melted. Spoon chocolate into prepared pan spreading evenly over bottom to within ½ inch of sides. Sprinkle with peppermint; press into chocolate.

3. Refrigerate until almost firm before cutting into squares. Refrigerate until firm before removing foil.

Makes about 3 dozen

Serving Suggestions: Peppermints are easier to cut into squares if chocolate is not completely firm. For a festive presentation, place individual candy pieces in paper or foil candy cups.

Santa's Peppermint Chocolates

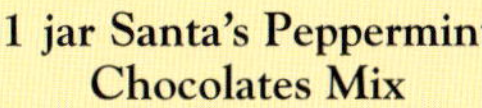

1 jar Santa's Peppermint Chocolates Mix

1. Line 8-inch square baking pan with buttered foil. Set aside.

2. Remove peppermint. Place remaining contents of jar in microwavable 2-cup glass measuring cup. Microwave on HIGH 1 to 2 minutes, stirring after every 30 seconds until chips are melted. Spoon chocolate into prepared pan spreading evenly over bottom to within ½ inch of sides. Sprinkle with peppermint; press into chocolate.

3. Refrigerate until almost firm before cutting into squares. Refrigerate until firm before removing foil.

Makes about 3 dozen

Serving Suggestions: Peppermints are easier to cut into squares if chocolate is not completely firm. For a festive presentation, place individual candy pieces in paper or foil candy cups.

Santa's Peppermint Chocolates

1 jar Santa's Peppermint Chocolates Mix

1. Line 8-inch square baking pan with buttered foil. Set aside.

2. Remove peppermint. Place remaining contents of jar in microwavable 2-cup glass measuring cup. Microwave on HIGH 1 to 2 minutes, stirring after every 30 seconds until chips are melted. Spoon chocolate into prepared pan spreading evenly over bottom to within ½ inch of sides. Sprinkle with peppermint; press into chocolate.

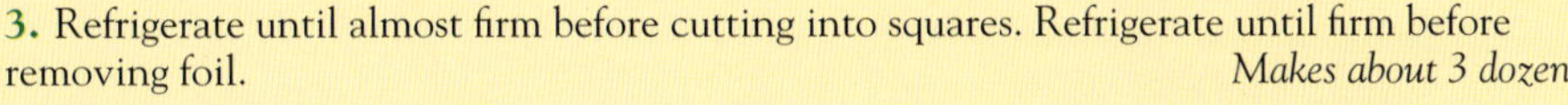

3. Refrigerate until almost firm before cutting into squares. Refrigerate until firm before removing foil.

Makes about 3 dozen

Serving Suggestions: Peppermints are easier to cut into squares if chocolate is not completely firm. For a festive presentation, place individual candy pieces in paper or foil candy cups.

Santa's Peppermint Chocolates

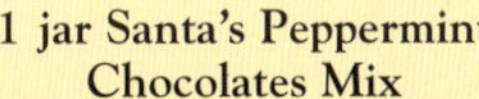

1 jar Santa's Peppermint Chocolates Mix

1. Line 8-inch square baking pan with buttered foil. Set aside.

2. Remove peppermint. Place remaining contents of jar in microwavable 2-cup glass measuring cup. Microwave on HIGH 1 to 2 minutes, stirring after every 30 seconds until chips are melted. Spoon chocolate into prepared pan spreading evenly over bottom to within ½ inch of sides. Sprinkle with peppermint; press into chocolate.

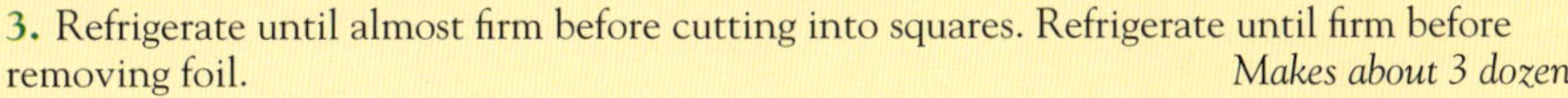

3. Refrigerate until almost firm before cutting into squares. Refrigerate until firm before removing foil.

Makes about 3 dozen

Serving Suggestions: Peppermints are easier to cut into squares if chocolate is not completely firm. For a festive presentation, place individual candy pieces in paper or foil candy cups.

Santa's Peppermint Chocolates

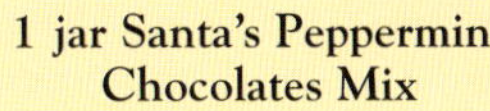

1 jar Santa's Peppermint Chocolates Mix

1. Line 8-inch square baking pan with buttered foil. Set aside.

2. Remove peppermint. Place remaining contents of jar in microwavable 2-cup glass measuring cup. Microwave on HIGH 1 to 2 minutes, stirring after every 30 seconds until chips are melted. Spoon chocolate into prepared pan spreading evenly over bottom to within ½ inch of sides. Sprinkle with peppermint; press into chocolate.

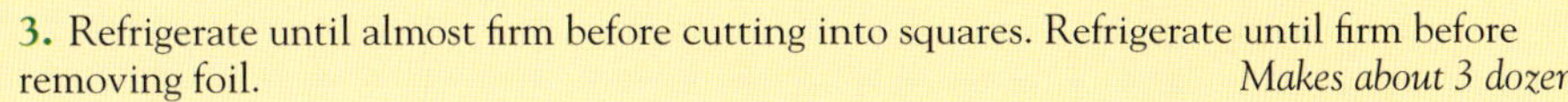

3. Refrigerate until almost firm before cutting into squares. Refrigerate until firm before removing foil.

Makes about 3 dozen

Serving Suggestions: Peppermints are easier to cut into squares if chocolate is not completely firm. For a festive presentation, place individual candy pieces in paper or foil candy cups.

Crispy Holiday Treats Mix

- 1 cup powdered sugar
- 1½ cups crisp rice cereal
- ½ cup chopped dried tart cherries
- ¾ cup mini semisweet chocolate chips
- ¼ cup chopped toasted pecans
- 1 cup flaked coconut

1. Layer all ingredients except coconut in the order listed above in 1-quart food storage jar with tight-fitting lid. Place coconut in small plastic food storage bag. Close with twist tie; cut off top of bag. Place bag in jar.
2. Cover top of jar with fabric; attach gift tag with raffia or ribbon.

Makes 1 (1-quart) jar

Crispy Holiday Treats

- 1 jar Crispy Holiday Treats Mix
- 1 cup peanut butter
- ¼ cup butter, softened

1. Remove coconut packet from jar. Place remaining contents of jar in large bowl; stir to blend. Combine peanut butter and butter in medium bowl, stirring until well blended. Add to cereal mixture. Stir until well blended.

2. Shape generous teaspoonfuls of dough into 1½-inch balls. Roll balls in coconut. Place in single layer in large food storage container. Store in refrigerator.

Makes about 2 dozen treats

Serving Suggestion: Place individual candies in paper or foil candy cups. Candy cups are available in a variety of designs and colors at stores which carry cake decorating supplies.

Crispy Holiday Treats

1 jar Crispy Holiday Treats Mix
1 cup peanut butter
¼ cup butter, softened

1. Remove coconut packet from jar. Place remaining contents of jar in large bowl; stir to blend. Combine peanut butter and butter in medium bowl, stirring until well blended. Add to cereal mixture. Stir until well blended.

2. Shape generous teaspoonfuls of dough into 1½-inch balls. Roll balls in coconut. Place in single layer in large food storage container. Store in refrigerator.

Makes about 2 dozen treats

Serving Suggestion: Place individual candies in paper or foil candy cups. Candy cups are available in a variety of designs and colors at stores which carry cake decorating supplies.

Crispy Holiday Treats

1 jar Crispy Holiday Treats Mix
1 cup peanut butter
¼ cup butter, softened

1. Remove coconut packet from jar. Place remaining contents of jar in large bowl; stir to blend. Combine peanut butter and butter in medium bowl, stirring until well blended. Add to cereal mixture. Stir until well blended.

2. Shape generous teaspoonfuls of dough into 1½-inch balls. Roll balls in coconut. Place in single layer in large food storage container. Store in refrigerator.

Makes about 2 dozen treats

Serving Suggestion: Place individual candies in paper or foil candy cups. Candy cups are available in a variety of designs and colors at stores which carry cake decorating supplies.

Crispy Holiday Treats

1 jar Crispy Holiday Treats Mix
1 cup peanut butter
¼ cup butter, softened

1. Remove coconut packet from jar. Place remaining contents of jar in large bowl; stir to blend. Combine peanut butter and butter in medium bowl, stirring until well blended. Add to cereal mixture. Stir until well blended.

2. Shape generous teaspoonfuls of dough into 1½-inch balls. Roll balls in coconut. Place in single layer in large food storage container. Store in refrigerator.

Makes about 2 dozen treats

Serving Suggestion: Place individual candies in paper or foil candy cups. Candy cups are available in a variety of designs and colors at stores which carry cake decorating supplies.

Crispy Holiday Treats

1 jar Crispy Holiday Treats Mix
1 cup peanut butter
¼ cup butter, softened

1. Remove coconut packet from jar. Place remaining contents of jar in large bowl; stir to blend. Combine peanut butter and butter in medium bowl, stirring until well blended. Add to cereal mixture. Stir until well blended.

2. Shape generous teaspoonfuls of dough into 1½-inch balls. Roll balls in coconut. Place in single layer in large food storage container. Store in refrigerator.

Makes about 2 dozen treats

Serving Suggestion: Place individual candies in paper or foil candy cups. Candy cups are available in a variety of designs and colors at stores which carry cake decorating supplies.

Crispy Holiday Treats

1 jar Crispy Holiday Treats Mix
1 cup peanut butter
¼ cup butter, softened

1. Remove coconut packet from jar. Place remaining contents of jar in large bowl; stir to blend. Combine peanut butter and butter in medium bowl, stirring until well blended. Add to cereal mixture. Stir until well blended.

2. Shape generous teaspoonfuls of dough into 1½-inch balls. Roll balls in coconut. Place in single layer in large food storage container. Store in refrigerator.

Makes about 2 dozen treats

Serving Suggestion: Place individual candies in paper or foil candy cups. Candy cups are available in a variety of designs and colors at stores which carry cake decorating supplies.

Crispy Holiday Treats

1 jar Crispy Holiday Treats Mix
1 cup peanut butter
¼ cup butter, softened

1. Remove coconut packet from jar. Place remaining contents of jar in large bowl; stir to blend. Combine peanut butter and butter in medium bowl, stirring until well blended. Add to cereal mixture. Stir until well blended.

2. Shape generous teaspoonfuls of dough into 1½-inch balls. Roll balls in coconut. Place in single layer in large food storage container. Store in refrigerator.

Makes about 2 dozen treats

Serving Suggestion: Place individual candies in paper or foil candy cups. Candy cups are available in a variety of designs and colors at stores which carry cake decorating supplies.